# AMERICAN
# INDIANS

## THE FIRST NATIONS

# AMERICAN INDIANS

## THE FIRST NATIONS

NATIVE NORTH AMERICAN LIFE, MYTH AND ART

LARRY J. ZIMMERMAN

DUNCAN BAIRD PUBLISHERS

LONDON

**AMERICAN INDIANS: THE FIRST NATIONS**

First published in the United Kingdom and Ireland in 2003
by Duncan Baird Publishers Ltd
Sixth Floor, Castle House
75–76 Wells Street
London W1T 3QH

Conceived, created and designed by Duncan Baird Publishers

**HALF-TITLE PAGE:** A Navajo sandpainting whose theme is that of protection.

**TITLE-VERSO PAGE:** A weather-beaten totem pole from the peoples of the Northwest Coast culture stands as a silent sentinel in Vancouver, British Columbia, Canada.

Project Editor: *Joanne Clay*
Project Designer: *Gail Jones*
Picture Editor: *Cecilia Weston-Baker*
Commissioned Artwork, decorative borders and map: *Neil Gower*
Commissioned Artwork Design: *Clare Thorpe*
Managing Editor: *Christopher Westhorp*
Managing Designer: *Dan Sturges*

ISBN: 1-904292-74-7

1 3 5 7 9 10 8 6 4 2

Typeset in Bernhard Modern, Perpetua and Shannon
Colour reproduction by Scanhouse, Malaysia
Printed and bound in Singapore by Imago

NOTES
The abbreviations CE and BCE are used throughout this book:
CE Common Era (the equivalent of AD)
BCE Before the Common Era (the equivalent of BC)

Any uncaptioned photographs are described on page 144.

# CONTENTS

**IMAGE AND
IMAGINATION  6**

The Soul of the Native
    North Americans  8

The Rocks that Teach  10

The Story of the Native
    North Americans  12

*Map: Culture Areas of Native
North America  13*

The Art of the Native
    North Americans  16

Invoking the Totem Spirits  18

Reclaiming the Past  20

Claiming the Present  22

**EVERYDAY LINKS
TO THE SACRED  24**

Wisdom Places  26

Spirit Bear's *Tipi*  28

To Protect Mother Earth  30

Mounds and Effigies  32

The Dome of the Sky  34

The Thunder Beings  36

Celestial Duality  38

Origins and Holy
    Landscapes  40

The Place of the Blue
    Smoke  44

Great Migrations  46

Space, Time, and the Divine  48

Cairns of the Arctic
    Giants  54

Ceremonial Chambers  56

Magnificent Dwellings of
    the Ancient Ones  58

**THE LIVING SPIRIT  60**

Spirits of Nature  62

Masks of Transformation  64

Ancestral Animals  66

As Swift as "Sky Dogs"  68

Totem and Clan  70

Raptor Messenger
    of the Sky Spirits  72

Heroes, Tricksters,
    and Monsters  74

Divine Protection and
    Power  78

Dream Voyages  80

Sacred Societies  82

Where *Manitous* Dwell  84

Even the Sacred Changes  86

**SYMBOL, MYTH,
AND COSMOS  88**

Earthdivers and World
    Makers  90

Circle of Time  92

The Unifying Circle  94

The Holiness of Artistry  96

Spider Woman's Blessing  100

Spirit Worlds  102

Hunters and Prey  104

Return of the Buffalo
    Nation  106

Gathering the Earth's
    Abundance  108

The Divine Gift
    of Maize  110

**RITUAL AND
SACRAMENT  112**

The Way of the
    Sacred Powers  114

Healing Ways  116

Seeking a Vision  118

Change, Renewal,
    and Dance  120

From Maiden to Changing
    Woman  124

Status of the Warriors  126

Adornment of the Brave  128

Exploits in Battle  130

Journey to the Afterlife  132

**Select List of Native
    Peoples and Regions  136**

**Further Reading  138**

**Index  139**

**Picture Credits  144**

# IMAGE AND IMAGINATION

**LEFT** Whereas the "more advanced" Europeans initially found life on the new continent difficult, Native North Americans were well adapted to their environment and felt at one with the landscape around them. Native people still celebrate this important and harmonious relationship with the earth at seasonal gatherings held across the continent.

When Europeans first set foot in North America, it was only to discover to their surprise that the continent already had human inhabitants. In fact, the indigenous people had prospered there; the population numbered as many as 20 million and cultures had developed that were as diverse as those anywhere on Earth. Many of the names the tribes had for themselves translated simply as "the people;" they were, and are, not all "Indians," but Inhanktonwan, Meskwaki, or Tohono O'odham. Ancient stories tell them who they are. Their long experience and the adaptation of their traditions during millennia of life in the so-called New World have helped them to survive—for Native North Americans are proudly people of *now*, not just back *then*.

**BELOW** The buffalo once played a fundamental role in the life of many native peoples, who saw the animal not only as a source of food and hide, but also as a sacred relative. Buffalo effigies similar to this ancient green quartzite one from the Plains region are still used during rituals and ceremonies that honor "The Buffalo Nation"—the name many native peoples use for the bison population.

# THE SOUL OF THE NATIVE NORTH AMERICANS

Native North Americans were a great puzzle to the first Europeans to arrive in the Americas. Where did these indigenous peoples come from? They were not mentioned in the Bible—did they have souls? Were they even human? The Christian Church finally declared in 1537 that the Indians were "children of God," but this did not prevent an onslaught against native ways of life. As exploration and contact expanded, diseases to which Indians had no immunity decimated populations and many of those who survived were displaced. Some attempts were made by the colonizers to exterminate native peoples, and there were concerted efforts to assimilate the rest. Yet, although a few groups such as the Beothuk of the Canadian Maritimes did literally disappear, most have endured. Drawing strength from their spiritual traditions, Indians have fought to maintain their cultures and have demonstrated both durability and adaptability in the face of adversity and pressure to change.

The adaptability of the First Peoples of North America was present well before Europeans arrived. The diversity of native cultures is the result of at least 12,000 years of successful accommodation to changes in both the natural and social environments. There were Native North American groups that practiced a partly nomadic lifestyle in which foraging for food was the norm, whereas others lived in permanent villages and practiced a mix of foraging and horticulture. Some cultures were high civilizations centered on sizeable settlements with large populations, which were dependent on crop growing. Some groups practiced animistic religions and had egalitarian social structures; others were almost theistic and had hierarchical social structures. As tribes moved around, they transformed those peoples with whom they came into contact, while simultaneously making adjustments to their own cultures to incorporate some of their new neighbors' traditions.

RIGHT Dancers at a powwow in Chehaw Park, Albany, Georgia. Large, secular tribal or intertribal get-togethers, known as powwows, provide important opportunities for the handing down of Indian traditions from one generation to the next.

What inspires and unites these different groups is a view of the world as a place of sacred mystery. The native relationship with the world is rooted in a profound respect for the land, its features and its life-forms. Mother Earth and Father Sky provide, but they also challenge. Humans are not above creation, but a part of it, and people must forge a respectful, balanced relationship with the world around them. The real soul of Native North Americans lies in these concepts, which have remained sufficiently powerful to enable their cultures to survive in the modern world.

### THE ROCKS THAT TEACH

Generations of people have left their mark on the North American landscape in the
form of thousands of boulder alignments, pictographs painted onto rock surfaces,
and petroglyphs pecked into rock—such as these rows of figures made by the
Anasazi (above) which can still be seen today on the Navajo Reservation. Rocks
with unusual shapes, colors, or positions were especially revered. Rock art usually
depicts sacred experiences—such as human-like beings (left, right, and opposite)—
or stylized renditions of the everyday—such as animals (above, left and right).
Many of these sites are still used by native people for expressing their spiritual
connections to the Earth.

# THE STORY OF THE NATIVE NORTH AMERICANS

Many Indian holy people and elders say that humans have inhabited North America since the dawn of time. However, the first Europeans to arrive on the continent were convinced that the Indians must have come from elsewhere— but where? Influenced by religion, there was speculation that they were descendants of the Lost Tribes of Israel. But since the discipline of archaeology developed in the

late 1880s, scholars have compiled less fanciful versions of the Native North Americans' story, although these have had to be revised each time that new evidence has come to light. As a result, many Indians discount the archaeological analysis of their history entirely.

By 1926 archaeologists had found incontrovertible evidence of an Indian presence in North America during the Ice Ages. This consisted of distinctive stone points designed to kill ancient bison and mammoth. It was believed that hunters had followed herds of wild animals from northeast Asia across Beringia, a land bridge between Siberia and Alaska. People had then penetrated southward into the Americas and by 10,000 years ago they were inhabiting every part of the northern hemisphere. Waves of immigration continued, even after the ice had melted and the sea had reclaimed the land bridge. The most recent of these arrivals—seafaring Asian Arctic people who were ancestors of the Inuit—settled the northern coasts of Alaska and Canada about 4,500 years ago. By the late 1960s there was good evidence that people had also traveled by boat along the Pacific coastline from Siberia. There are even suggestions that people may have come around the Pacific Rim and the northern Atlantic Ocean ice.

By whichever means they may have arrived, there is no doubt that Native North Americans were firmly established on the continent 10,000 years ago. As their

LEFT *Young Omaha, War Eagle, Little Missouri, and Pawnees*, **painted in 1821 by Charles Bird King (1785–1862). He is best known for his portraits of Native American dignitaries who traveled to Washington, DC, to confer with US government officials. King's paintings were published in a** *History of the Indian Tribes of North America between 1836 and 1844* **by Thomas L. McKenney (1785–1859).**

# CULTURE AREAS OF NATIVE NORTH AMERICA

BEAUFORT SEA

*Yukon River*

Baffin Island

LABRADOR SEA

*Mackenzie River*

9

*Great Slave Lake*

8

Hudson Bay

ROCKY MOUNTAINS

7

5

Lake Superior

8

*St. Lawrence River*

Lake Huron

Lake Ontario

1

*Snake River*

*Missouri River*

*Mississippi River*

Lake Erie

Lake Michigan

6

*Colorado River*

4

2

1

Ohio River

APPALACHIANS

3

*Rio Grande*

**1** Eastern Woodlands

**2** Great Plains

**3** Southwest

**4** Great Basin

**5** Plateau

**6** California

**7** Northwest Coast

**8** Sub-Arctic

**9** Arctic

populations grew, people began to settle along river drainages, where they survived by hunting and gathering. Groups in more difficult environments continued this way of life until the Europeans came; elsewhere, other native peoples adapted to their surroundings by developing domesticated plants, the most notable of which were maize, beans, and squashes—the Three Sisters (see page 108). The benefits of crop surpluses included the freedom they afforded for some individuals to become specialists in religion and governance. By the first century CE, trade networks had started moving materials such as stone for tools and shells for ornamentation across lands east of the Rocky Mountains. Earthworks appeared, both for burial and ceremony. Native groups developed more complex religious beliefs, and languages multiplied. By about 800CE cities had grown up that were based around social hierarchies such as chiefdoms.

The fact that the Indians had spent thousands of years successfully adapting to natural environments is reflected in the culture-area concept, a scheme first developed by anthropologists in the 1930s and still used today by almost everyone in discussing Native North Americans (see map, page 13). The idea of culture areas derives from the fact that Indian cultures reflected the environment in which peoples had lived for most of their history. The precise names for regions varies, but usually includes the Eastern Woodlands (northeastern and southeastern), the Great Plains, the Arctic, the Sub-Arctic, the Northwest Coast, the Plateau, the Great Basin, the Southwest, and California—each area having distinctive patterns of food production, social organization, religion, and material culture.

However, this was all to be disrupted after 1492CE when Christopher Columbus "discovered" the Americas. Displaced by encroaching European settlement, groups of Natives were pushed into the territories of other Indian nations, which increased intertribal contact and exacerbated conflicts. As a result, the culture-area patterns began to break down. (Modern scholars recognize that the model, while useful for the pre-Contact era, fails to take into account Indians' continuing adaptability.) Put onto reservations, Native North Americans were subjected to broken treaties, "missionizing" by Christian prosetylizers, the repression of indigenous religion, land swindling, and a general cultural onslaught that continued well into the 1970s. By 1890, most North Americans agreed that Indians were bound to become extinct, or to be absorbed into the social mainstream. Yet native people survived, in spite of it all. Many threats remain, but economic and legal structures have shifted, and there has recently been a resurgence of native numbers and traditions. Indians are a people of today, not just of yesterday.

LEFT **After crossing Beringia from Siberia, many native peoples passed through Alaska and gradually migrated southward. However, some groups stayed and settled this icy landscape, most of them surviving by hunting, fishing, and foraging in small family bands.**

BELOW **The Inuit created snow goggles such as this ancient pair to protect them from snow blindness caused by the glare of the sun on the ice in the frozen north, the first region on the continent to be encountered by humans.**

# THE ART OF THE NATIVE NORTH AMERICANS

The earliest human artifacts found in the Americas are stone tools, many of them points for spears and lances, designed to kill Ice Age animals. Made from stone selected for its strength and beauty, many of the tools are exquisite in form, with parallel flake scars from edge to edge. Like these first tools, much of Native North American art reflects elements of the different environments in which people live, combining animistic spirit with physical object—even the spirit of the stone is considered. Art is an essential ingredient of everyday objects: stone tools, pottery, and basketry are expressions of their creators' lives and cosmologies.

Materials often affected the form of designs within culture areas, but the content usually reflected spiritual outlook. Peoples of the Plains worked with flattened porcupine quills and later with glass trade beads, which tended to limit designs to geometric forms; in the Southwest, the Great Basin, and California, extraordinary baskets were similarly embellished. Working with paints, wood and ceramics allowed greater flexibility—but even here, what was important in life was what became important as representational artistic motifs. Northwest Coast peoples carved and painted portrayals of clan totems on wood (see pages 18–19). Southwestern and Eastern Woodlands tribes decorated pottery with complex human and animal forms.

Performance arts, such as music, storytelling, and dance, also reflected the Indians' environment, daily life, and world views. These activities transmitted knowledge and lifted the spirit, as well as providing a means of creative expression.

Contemporary Native North American artists maintain continuity with the artistic traditions of the past, in some cases even reviving nearly vanished skills, but at the same time artists often experiment with modern materials and themes. Indian painting and sculpture were never absent, but have flourished since the

**RIGHT Traditional Southwestern basketry employs a range of roots and grasses that make full use of contrasting coloration in the natural fibers to provide a variety of bold patterns. Basketmaking remains principally a craft activity of women.**

1940s, and can now be found in major art collections and exhibitions. Native dance and theater companies, most of them intertribal, tour the world. Music by Indian performers and composers has found its way into the mainstream. Native North American literature expands the tradition of storytelling. Many of the themes are traditional, but new ones incorporate native experiences after Contact—some are angry and some conciliatory, yet all are exploring what it now means to be Indian.

## INVOKING THE TOTEM SPIRITS

The peoples of the Northwest Coast honored the totem animals of their clans by incorporating them as family crests in almost all their carving, weaving, or painting. Neither the images nor the creatures they represent were worshiped, but instead marked a family's history and powers, thereby linking clans to the distant times of myth. Northwest Coast art is visually stunning and executed with bold colors such as red, black, and orange. Animals are the main subject, but sometimes botanical and celestial themes are used. Most of the art is representational rather than realistic, portraying the animal's salient attributes in stylized ways. The visual field is usually filled, leaving little open space, which according to some scholars indicates a hierarchically structured society.

This traditional design has been painted onto the end of a large cedar plank house, known as a "big house." Each of these buildings was large enough to shelter several families and their possessions, provide workspace, and accommodate visitors for a ritual, a feast, or a potlatch. In the painting are several birds, including the dominant figure occupying the top, with its head, beak, wing, and talons represented. There are also heads of small birds in the lower left and upper right corners. Outsiders often find it difficult to tell eagles, thunderbirds, and ravens apart; however, this is not a problem for the local residents, who know from the clan's name and reputation which animal totem spirits are depicted in such designs.

# RECLAIMING THE PAST

In the face of the European and American onslaught, Native North Americans were overwhelmed and reduced to seeking survival just by holding onto their identity. Nations were often obliged to cede the right to their homeland, and many were forcibly removed into unfamiliar territories (see pages 44–45). Countless deaths due to disease, warfare, and maltreatment challenged the very core of most Native North American societies. Indians became objects of scientific curiosity; their bones were collected from battlefields and burial grounds for study.

For most non-Indians, if the indigenous people did not succumb to policies of assimilation they simply became "invisible." This situation began to abate in the 1930s, when more Native North Americans were included in the United States federal government to run Indian affairs, but even then the government tried to terminate federal recognition and assistance—a disaster for the tribes. However, with the Civil Rights movements of the late 1960s, Indian activist organizations such as the American Indian Movement began to raise awareness about Indian problems. Efforts to recover lands or secure compensation for broken treaties have since found their way to the US courts, where the Lakota, Nakota, and Dakota (Sioux) are still trying to regain lands from their sacred territory of Paha Sapa (the Black Hills). A victory of another sort was achieved in 1990 with the Native American Graves Protection and Repatriation Act, which demanded that human remains and burial goods, as well as sacred objects held by federal institutions, be returned to affiliated tribes.

Similar land and cultural-rights disputes are being played out in Canada. In 1999 the Inuit-controlled territory of Nunavut ("Our Land" in the Inuit language), where eighty-five per cent of the population is Inuit, was established. In both the US and Canada First Peoples are also struggling to save their rapidly disappearing languages by establishing tribal schools in which native language and culture are taught.

# CLAIMING THE PRESENT

Although reclaiming the past has become important to many Native North Americans, tribes are now also concentrating on overcoming the problems of everyday life. Economic hardship is a major issue: many of the United States reservations and Canadian reserves were purposely set up in desolate areas, and many have few resources of any kind. However, some have excellent natural resources, such as timber and mineral wealth, but these assets are either undeveloped or are not under the native people's direct control. In both countries, sovereignty and rights established by treaties are sources of a great deal of debate.

LEFT  In an effort to link past and present, the handprints on the wall of this modern building on the Lakota reservation at Pine Ridge, South Dakota, are reminiscent of designs that were painted on *tipi* covers in the 19th century.

Much of the activism of the 1970s and later has been geared toward self-determination in daily life, not merely claiming identity and heritage. With the energy crisis of the early 1970s, mineral wealth found on reservation lands provided jobs and capital for a few tribes. In the US, the most significant economic advance was the development of casinos by a number of tribes, which was permitted by the Indian Gaming Regulatory Act of 1978. By 2000, just over 100 of the 500 recognized tribes had viable casinos, and profit sharing of this income has finally provided tribes with a decent standard of living for their peoples, enabling them to improve their infrastructure, including better housing, roads, medical care, and schools. The Meskwaki and Ojibwe have used revenues to buy back tribal lands, and a number of these purchases have been put to traditional uses, such as sustaining the wild rice crop. Organizations such as the Great Lakes Indian Fish and Wildlife Commission work toward the conservation of resources and public education about treaty rights and Indian ecology.

In both the US and Canada, tribal education programs have blossomed, with schools teaching tribal languages alongside the skills needed in non-Indian society, extending from elementary to university education. Growing numbers of Indian people enter professional and scholarly fields, so that medicine and law can be practiced in ways more in concert with traditional values. Legal challenges relating to religious freedom appear regularly in the courts. In particular, the protection of sacred sites in the face of land development requires constant vigilance.

To say that American Indians and Canada's First Peoples are winning all these battles would be naive, but today the outlook is at least positive for the first time in generations. This very struggle for cultural autonomy may be one key to understanding what it means to be a Native North American.

ABOVE **For some Indian tribes, the production and sale of traditionally inspired craft objects, such as these silver thunderbird earrings with turquoise insets and beadwork, have helped both to preserve native artistry skills and to provide the group with a source of income.**

# EVERYDAY LINKS TO THE SACRED

Shawnee Chief Tecumseh once declared: "The earth is my mother and on her bosom I will repose." Spoken in 1810, his elegant words echo through time, an expression of a core belief for most Native North American cultures. Mother Earth takes many forms. She provides everything to sustain life and more: she is the nurturer. She is a point of origin and a point of completion. As the Ojibwe say: "Woman is forever, eternal: man comes from woman and to woman he returns." She is where the bones of the ancestors rest. Everything within the landscape reminds the people of her, and their identity reflects her features. Mother Earth is both the everyday and the sacred; she is to be both cherished and respected.

# WISDOM PLACES

According to the Cibecue Apache, "Wisdom sits in places." Many American Indian tribes believe that they are inseparable from the landscape, sharing a spatial concept of history in which the temporal elements are of secondary importance to knowing "the significance of here." Whether it involves a knowledge of sacred history, being able to locate important natural resources, or having an intimate understanding of one's place in the grand scheme of existence, the wisdom that imbues major sites lies at the very foundation of the Indian world view.

LEFT **Bear Butte, South Dakota, is a sacred location for many Indian groups, especially the Kiowa, Cheyenne, and Lakota, who come here to seek visions. Tokens of the prayers that are made during sweat-lodge rituals are often left fastened to trees. Red cloth represents an offering to the sun, green to the Earth, and blue to the sky.**

Each native group knows its landscape intimately. For nomadic tribes, such as the Dogrib of northwestern Canada, the land is crossed by trails that are used all year round (see pages 54–55). Thousands of places have a unique story that provides the means to navigate the region. The names of wisdom places often relate to key resources that can be found there: for example, Blood Rock is known as the birthplace of Yamosh, a Dogrib culture hero, but it is also where the Dogrib quarry a red stone that is used to produce tools for killing and processing animals, and this makes the location vital to the tribe's survival.

Sites can become important because of their unusual appearance, as with the skull-shaped Blood Rock, or because they were once the site of a cataclysmic event, such as an earthquake. Places at a high altitude are closer to the juncture of earth and sky, and it is therefore thought that certain spirits may be more accessible here. The Acumawi people say that a spring on Mount Shasta in northern California contains the tears of all the deer, so that deer won't cry out when killed by hunters. Some places become intertwined with oral tradition and tribal myth because "history," and thus the tribe's "character," is thought to have originated there. Wind Cave in the southern Black Hills is where the Lakota people were tricked by the spider Iktomi into emerging. Bear Butte (see illustration, opposite) on the edge of the northern Black Hills is where the Cheyenne culture hero Sweet Medicine received the four sacred arrows that brought blessings to his people.

Wisdom places have many uses: some are where holy people conduct their rituals or where individuals seek a vision (see pages 118–119); others may be sites of pilgrimage for specific clans or whole tribes. Although some shrines exist, more often people simly leave offerings such as tobacco in a natural setting. Wisdom places are varied in form and associated belief, yet the single, overarching theme that unites them is that they provide a people with its identity.

### SPIRIT BEAR'S *TIPI*

The mysterious rock formation of Devil's Tower in Wyoming is known to more than twenty native tribes by a variety of names, but the Crow, Lakota, Kiowa, Arapaho, and Cheyenne all share similar tales about its origins. Mato Tipila ("Bear's *Tipi*" in Lakota) is said to be the lair of a large grizzly bear. Some Indian stories tell how Bear was chasing seven sisters and the rock grew upward in order to carry them to safety, out of his reach. In frustration, Bear tried to climb the rock—

the marks visible on the sides of the stone were made by his claws—but the sisters eluded him and later became the seven stars of the Pleiades star cluster. Cheyenne narratives say that the rock is where their culture hero Sweet Medicine had a vision as he lay dying—one that predicted the disappearance of the buffalo, the coming of the horse, and the impact of the white man. Local tribes still hold rituals, such as sweat-lodge ceremonies, vision quests, and Sun Dances, near Mato Tipila, and used to conduct funerals there.

# TO PROTECT MOTHER EARTH

Almost from the beginning, Indians have been stereotyped as being close to nature, or "noble savages." In recent years native people have been labeled the "first ecologists." Protecting the land is part of daily life, and many see it as a limitless responsibility. In fact, Indians are ecological in the truest sense—they know nature's cycles and understand its tolerances; they see themselves as a part of the land itself, no better than the other creatures that live on it. To Native Americans, ecology is a matter of balance and respect.

Indians have had to pay careful attention to the land's ability to sustain them. Hunting and gathering peoples, especially in areas where there were limited resources, understood that they needed to keep their own population levels low, and human populations were usually maintained at about ten percent of the number the land could sustain. The Mistassini Cree hunters around what is now called Hudson's Bay kept a record of the animals they took so that they did not overhunt. If the Cree thought game numbers were declining. they moved into hunting territories that had not been exploited recently. Similarly, farming tribes, such as the Mandan and Hidatsa, knew that the land could only sustain crops for a few seasons before it needed fallow time. Because eagle feathers were an important part of rituals, many tribes took care to protect local populations of these sacred and rare birds. This was done by building eagle-trapping lodges—when an eagle landed there, hunters held its legs and plucked a few feathers before releasing it.

This harmony between humans and nature changed radically when Europeans settled North America. By the late 1800s, the buffalo had almost been exterminated. Tribal lands have been cleared of forests and waters have been polluted. Many Indians have stepped forward to speak out against this desecration and have become eloquent spokespeople for a range of contemporary environmental causes.

RIGHT This "black-fish" mask was made among the Yupik of the lower Yukon to represent the many-toothed *qacullut*, or wolf fish. Animal masks were often worn by Native North American hunters when taking part in ritual dances in order to appease an animal's spirit before they hunted it down. Such shows of respect were a fundamental part of the Indians' relationship with their environment and its life-forms.

# MOUNDS AND EFFIGIES

Mother Earth's countless hills and mountains rise toward the heavens and mark important places where Indians can go to touch both the earth and sky. Native people everywhere seem to seek out these elevated places, and have sometimes created them. Among the earliest examples of this in North America were the mounds built from around 1000BCE by Indians east of the Rocky Mountains. Many more such mounds—which were used to bury the dead, to mark clan territories, and to serve as platforms for temples—later appeared all over the Woodlands and Plains. By the time they were surveyed in the nineteenth century, many mounds had been destroyed, although in 1890 around 10,000 remained.

Burial mounds are generally conical or linear. Conical mounds are cone-shaped, though rounded on top, and sometimes more elliptical than round at the base. Linear mounds tend to be long and narrow. Burial mounds vary in size: their diameter or length ranges from just a few feet to more than 100 feet (30 meters); their height varies from about 3 feet (1 meter) to more than 30 feet (10 meters). Such mounds often contained the remains of more than one individual, perhaps many members of the same clan, placed in the mound at different times. In some cases mounds were built over many years as more bodies and baskets of soil were

LEFT **An effigy pipe from the Hopewell Culture (ca. 300BCE–500CE). Items such as this were interred with the deceased and have frequently been recovered from burial mounds. Frogs or toads were often represented, possibly because of symbolic primal associations of metamorphosis and emergence from water.**

RIGHT **The Great Serpent Mound in Ohio appears to have been built by the Adena, Hopewell, or the later Fort Ancient cultures between 800CE and 1500CE. The earthen effigy is 4 feet (1.2m) high, 20 feet (6m) wide, and more than 1,250 feet (381m) long. At its open mouth is an oval mound, or "egg," being swallowed, perhaps to represent a solar eclipse. Eastern Woodland culture has long associations with snakes and the underworld.**

added. The recently deceased would normally be buried in the mound in an extended or flexed (fetal) position, but sometimes bodies were placed on scaffolds open to the sky and only after the bones had fallen to the ground were they picked up, placed in a bundle and then buried in the mound.

Geometric and effigy mounds were important variations on the theme. In some cases, burial mounds were accompanied by large enclosures with multiple ridges of earth, in circular, octagonal, or square shapes. Effigy mounds, most of which were built ca. 650CE–1100CE, contain no burials, and given their location on ridgelines it is thought that they may have marked clans' territorial boundaries. These mounds tend to be about 3 feet (1 meter) high and are shaped like creatures, such as bears, birds, or panthers. Most surviving effigy mounds can be seen along the hills and ridges of the Mississippi River where the modern states of Iowa, Minnesota, Illinois, and Wisconsin come together. On one terrace above Brush Creek in Adams County, Ohio, a spectacular, long, serpentine earthwork known as the Great Serpent Mound (see illustration, above) loops its way along a bluff.

By 1200CE, probably influenced by cultures from Central America, some groups began to construct platform mounds, most of which appear along the Mississippi River and its tributaries in the southeastern culture area. These mounds were truncated earthen pyramids crowned by a temple. Platform mounds were sites of important rituals that helped sustain the world and the social order.

# THE DOME OF THE SKY

If Native North Americans are influenced by the landscape around them, they are also constantly aware of the sky overhead. From the heavens comes the weather—life-giving rains, snow, thunder, and the winds of every season. Interaction with the firmament is inescapable, and people take care to heed its many messages. On an everyday level, by watching the sky Indians are able to see bad weather coming and take proper action—but the supernatural is never far away; the Koyukon, for example, regard thunderstorms as transformations of a human spirit from the Distant Time. Storms are believed to possess awareness and can therefore be influenced; a Koyukon hunter might pinch a female dog so that her yelp scares away the storm, or paint a red circle on his paddle and wave it toward the west as the dark clouds approach, ordering the storm to go out to the coast.

The sky is a place of both origins and endings—a domain inhabited by many beings, some benevolent and some wicked. For the Netsilik, an Inuit people of Pelly Bay in Arctic Canada, the sky is the home of Narssuk, a weather god who takes the form of a strong and malevolent giant baby. Wrapped in caribou skins tied with thongs, he is a wicked spirit who detests humans. Whenever Narssuk gets loose, a blizzard is unleashed. In order to restore good weather, shamans have to enter a trance state and ascend into the sky to fight Narssuk, then retie his loosened thongs. Tatqeq, on the other hand, is a gentle, people-loving moon spirit who has little power but brings luck to hunters and fertility to women.

The night sky is a source of important information. In the risings of stars, Native North Americans looked for patterns to indicate the shifts of seasons that are so crucial to planting. Relatively rare celestial events such as eclipses, comets, or supernovas might be read as good or bad omens, requiring special rituals to be held either in celebration or to forestall evil. However, most celestial events form a

dependable phase and certain ritual cycles were keyed to star movements. Sheet lightning and low, rumbling thunder starting in the west and rolling around the entire sky, combined with the proper position for the Pleiades, represent significant milestones for the Skidi Pawnee. This announces the transition between winter and summer, reproducing the creation of the world in miniature and signalling that it is time for the Evening Star bundle ceremonies. The Skidi Pawnee believe in intimate relation-ships between themselves and celes-tial objects: fixed stars are thought to have great power—they even created people and gave each band of the tribe a medicine bundle. The stars are either gods (see caption, right) or people who have become stars.

Heavenly bodies are usually male or female. Day brings the male sun and light; night the female moon, stars, and darkness. For the Omaha, the Inshta-thuda, or Sky People, are the counterparts of the Hon'gashenu, the Earth People. These two groups together form a circle that reflects the Omaha idea that cre-ation is ongoing through the union of male and female.

**LEFT** The Skidi Pawnee had a significantly developed tribal cosmogony, which is reflected in this hide chart of the night sky, used in divination. The historic Pawnee believed their villages had been founded by particular stars, and the most important gods remain the red, male star of the east, known as the Morning Star, and the bright, white, female star of the west, known as the Evening Star—both being, in reality, the planet Venus.

# THE THUNDER BEINGS

There are places that are said to possess a voice with a sound like thunder or crashing waters. Believed to exist at a juncture between the sky and either the earth, the seas, or the forests, such sites derive their unsettling aural effects from the fact that they are inhabited by thunder beings. These elemental entities feature in the lore of most tribes, but are understood in a divergent number of ways. Thunder beings can be both creative and destructive and are usually associated with violent weather—especially lightning, wind, and rain. Because of this, they are often linked with the west, the direction from which most storms come.

The exact residence of these beings varies but commonly it is significant as a site of immense energy; this may be a general location in the sky, to the west, or in the mountains. It may be where the creator lives or came from, the place where culture heroes and tricksters went for inspiration, or to which they returned after their work was done—or it may be a particular mountain or body of water at the very source of life itself. For example, the Iroquois identify the sound of Niagara Falls (see caption, opposite) as the voice of the thunder being they call the water spirit. According to the Lakota, parts of sacred Paha Sapa once thundered mysteriously, a phenomenon that ended when the mining of gold began there. These hills are also home to Wakinyan, the Lakota form of the thunderbird, which is said to live at the top of Harney Peak, near

LEFT **Made by the Coast Salish Indians of the Northwest Coast, this spindle whorl is an everyday object that has been embellished with the majestic figure of a thunderbird, which carries a salmon in its talons.**

Wind Cave where the Lakota themselves first emerged from under the ground. Wakinyan's voice is said to be the thunderclap, and the rolling thunder that follows are the voices of his children, the thunderbirds. A glance of his eye can cause lightning. In North Carolina it is mountainous terrain once again that provides a home for native thunder beings—Red Man, who can be found at Pilot Mountain, which is known to the Cherokee as Tsuwatelda. The name Red Man is due to his beautiful dress of lightning and rainbows. He and his two sons, who introduced the Cherokee to the gift of fire, can be helpful provided that the people pray to them.

LEFT **The roar of Niagara Falls (from Nee-ah-gah-rah, which means "thundering waters") was said to be that of the spirit in its waters, which was appeased annually by sacrifices. The Iroquois explain how the "horseshoe" of the falls was formed when the basin was scooped out by the thrashing of a giant serpent killed by a thunderbolt sent by a good spirit from Lake Ontario.**

## CELESTIAL DUALITY

Native North Americans watch the sky attentively and have many stories to account

for the origins of celestial objects. For most tribes, the heavenly bodies of the sun

and the moon represent the dualities of creation, such as life/death, man/woman,

and good/evil. The unchanging sun and the variable moon are used to represent

phases of the cycle of existence. Tribes revere the sun and moon by incorporating

them into different aspects of culture, from housing—the roundness of a *tipi* (above)

simulates the sacred circle of the cosmos—to ritual objects, such as this Ghost Dance

drum (opposite, left), decorated with heavenly bodies, and a Hopi priest's buckskin

shield (opposite, right) in the form of a rising sun.

# ORIGINS AND
# HOLY LANDSCAPES

Whereas the Judeo-Christian tradition has a creator God who makes human beings in his own image and gives them dominion over the Earth, most Native North American origin stories give people no more power than the other parts of creation, whether animate or inanimate. People are the Earth's partners and know it intimately as the source from which they sprang. The lands on which Indians live reflect the creation, and there is a rich body of stories that detail how things came to be. The places where peoples are believed to have made their first appearance are always revered and sacred, and the accompanying tales typically contain

elements of the mythical intertwined with the real. Such stories of origins and land-scapes are more numerous than the tribes. Taken together they constitute a canon of themes in which the complex relations between land, weather, plants, animals, and people are described. The land is filled with mystery and power—it has existed since the beginning of time and will last for as long as the people are there to tell the stories.

Many origin stories describe native people as coming from a dark place—some emerge from beneath the ground, others from under the waters. Some experts have suggested that this dark place is an allegory for being born, of passing through the birth canal into the light. Others have suggested that it may refer to the Beringia land bridge, a place held in folk memory from the time of the great waves of migration into the Americas during the somber seasons of the Arctic year in the last Ice Age (see page 12). However, most Native North Americans take creation stories more literally and list precise sites as their people's point of origin.

Despite their linguistic differences, all the Puebloan peoples of the Southwest have a similar term to denote the place of origin: for Keresan-speakers, such as the community of Acoma, it is *sipap*, for the Uto-Aztecan-speaking Hopi it is *sipapu*, and for the Tanoan-speaking Tewa it is *sipophene*. The actual location of *sipophene* was a dark realm beneath Sandy Place Lake far to the north, where people, animals, and supernatural beings lived together as immortals. The Corn Mothers of the Tewa asked a man to find a way for the people to leave the lake. Eventually persuaded to explore the surface, the man went to the four directions, only to find mist and haze. He returned saying that he had seen the world and that it was *ochu*, meaning green or unripe. The second time he went into the world, he encountered fierce animals but they eventually became his friends and sent him back bearing gifts. The people rejoiced, saying, "we have been accepted," and followed the man to the lake's sur-face—and the area where they emerged is enclosed by four sacred mountains and

LEFT **A storm gathers over the Badlands, South Dakota. The Badlands hold great spiritual significance for several native peoples, including the Lakota, whose legends relate that this place was once the site of a primeval cataclysmic struggle during which giant monsters were slain (see page 103).**

four sacred hills. For the Hopi, who came into the world in a similar way near the Grand Canyon's Colorado River, the underworld emergence place is commemorated by an opening on the floor of a ceremonial *kiva* (see pages 56–57).

Familiar themes to these appear among the origin stories of the neighboring Navajo, who emphasize the great power that certain places derive from their links to the creation. According to the Navajo, the holy people created First Man and First Woman, who journeyed through several dark underworlds before emerging through a hollow reed. First Man stored soil in his medicine bundle, along with other magical substances, and from this soil the couple created four sacred mountains in what is now the Four Corners area where four states meet. In the east they pinned down Blanco Peak with a bolt of lightning and covered it with a blanket of daylight; in the south Mount Taylor was held down by a stone knife and topped with blue; in the west the San Francisco Peaks were draped with yellow and secured with a sunbeam; and in the north a rainbow bound Hesperus Peak, and First Man and First Woman then covered it with darkness. Each peak, direction, and color became associated with special powers: white lightning in the east; blue sky in the south; yellow for the sun in the west; and black for the storm clouds to the north. Atop Gobernador Knob in New Mexico, First Man and First Woman found Changing Woman, who begot the Navajo people by mixing her skin with water and corn.

The same powerful sense of a rootedness in place can be found at the other end of the continent. On a peninsula near Georgian Bay in southern Ontario live the Huron. They call themselves the Wendat, which is usually translated as "Dwellers in a Peninsula" or "the Islanders." While this may refer to the Huron's traditional homeland, it also reflects their belief that the Earth is an island on the back of a turtle. In Wisconsin, all the clans of the Winnebago, or Ho-Chunk, claim to be from an area close to the Red Banks near Green Bay in Lake Michigan. The Bear Clan's

creation story tells of a bear that came walking across the ocean, which upon reaching the shore became a raven and a gathering of all the clans was held at the spot.

The role of animals is a common theme. The Yokut in California say that the land was once covered with floodwater, and Eagle and Crow were perched on a

stump wondering how they could get it to return. Duck came along, dived to the bottom and brought up mud on his bill, which Eagle and Crow scraped off to make two big piles. The pair each rewarded Duck with a fish, but Eagle's pile of mud grew faster because he then gave Duck two fish. Crow's pile became the Coast Mountain Range, while Eagle's turned into the majestic Sierra Nevada.

In Alaska, the Aleut relate what happened after Raven had secured daylight (see caption, right). A man and woman came down from the sky in a bladder, which they stretched until it became land. The man scattered his hair, and trees and animals sprang up. The woman made the seas by urinating, and created the lakes and rivers by spitting into ditches and holes. Chips of wood were thrown into the river to make fish. Their firstborn son played with a stone which became an island. Another of their sons and a female dog were placed on the island and set afloat. This became Kodiak Island, and the Kodiak people who inhabit it believe they are the descendants of that son and his dog-wife.

LEFT **A Tlingit headdress depicting a semi-human Raven clutching the box of daylight, represented by the inlaid mirror. In common with other northern peoples such as the Aleut, the Tlingit of the Northwest Coast believe that Raven brought daylight to the first people by stealing a box in which the sun, moon, and stars had been hoarded by a rich man. Raven stole the box from its island hiding place near Sitka, Alaska, and set the light free.**

## THE PLACE OF THE BLUE SMOKE

The Cherokee use a word, *eloheh*, for land, which also means history, culture, and religion. It emphasizes how the people conceive of themselves as inseparable from their homeland. However, the history of the Cherokee is a tragic one of displacement and forced relocation. Related by language to the Iroquois of the north, the seven clans of the Cherokee are believed to have migrated southward to the Smoky Mountains of North Carolina, where they settled around 1000CE. Over time they came to regard this as their sacred, ancestral realm.

By the time of European colonization, from the 1700s on, the Cherokee probably numbered approximately 25,000 and were spread across what are now eight states. In 1827 gold was found by settlers on some Cherokee lands and the authorities began to confiscate territory. A decade later, the Cherokee were forcibly removed to land in the west that the government had designated as Indian Territory, in what is now Oklahoma. This transfer took place during the brutal winter of 1838–1839, and out of the 16,000 who made the journey along the Trail of Tears, about a quarter died. A few thousand resisted and hid out in their mountainous domain. In 1865, the state of North Carolina assured the permanent residence of the Cherokee on the Qualla Indian Reservation in the Smoky Mountains. The Cherokee know this homeland as Shaconage, or "place of blue smoke," in reference to the spectacular mists caused by the pine oil and water vapor emitted by the vegetation.

# GREAT MIGRATIONS

According to anthropologists, scientific evidence confirms that the origins of the Indians in the Americas are ancient and migratory (see page 12). The native peoples, though, have their own stories about where they came from, and most believe that they were created in North America, even if in their oral histories some groups acknowledge great historical mobility within the continent.

Whatever one chooses to believe, there is little doubt that many Indian tribes were constantly on the move, often as the result of environmental factors, over-population, or conflict with other groups already resident in a particular region.

**RIGHT The warlike ferocity of a Choctaw ball game is captured in this painting by George Catlin (1794–1872), who traveled to record everyday life among the Five Civilized Tribes (Cherokee, Chickasaw, Choctaw, Creek, and Seminole). Catlin observed this scene in Oklahoma (from the Choctaw for "red people"—their translation of Indian Territory) after the Choctaw had been forcibly removed eastward along the Trail of Tears.**

Such migrations did not always involve one mass movement, but often were a kind of trickle of people from one place to the next. As they spread from area to area, tribes evolved culturally, but usually retained a few ties with their original culture.

Good examples of this process are the Navajo and Apache, two groups that we classify as Southwestern. However, like all Indians, they are the end-product of a migration that began in Asia several thousand years ago. The Navajo's origin story—which describes their ascent to the surface and the miracles that led to the establishment of the traditional Navajo way of life around 1400CE—is an allegory for the Athapascan migration that links tribes from the Arctic to Mexico through their roots in a common language family. Similarities are evident between the Navajo tongue and those of the Haida and Tlingit peoples of the Northwest Coast and the Hupa and Mattole of northern California, as well as their Apache neighbors. Although anthropologists and linguists can often trace the movement of peoples in this way (through language remnants, parts of stories, and similarities in ritual), tribes themselves often have only vague information about their past because the process was slow and the details have been lost over time. The Navajo, for example, claim they were created in the Southwest and do not believe other accounts.

Sadly, there were migrations after Contact that were involuntary. Groups which had been living somewhere for centuries were pushed off their lands. The Meskwaki (Fox) started their journey along the east coast, were forced into Indian Territory in the west, then returned to Iowa by buying back land for a settlement. The Northern Cheyenne were removed from Montana to Indian Territory, only to escape back home after fighting a running battle across the Plains in 1878–79. Such forced migration changed cultures profoundly. Groups were thrown into contact with tribes of wholly different backgrounds, which sometimes led to conflict, but just as often it resulted in a hybridization of cultural practices.

# SPACE, TIME, AND THE DIVINE

Indian cultures were not as timeless and unchanging as commonplace perceptions would suggest. As with any living culture, changes took place in reaction to different natural and social environments. Native North Americans have always made creative use of the resources that Mother Earth provides, and over the millennia populations flourished wherever the environment allowed. People experimented with the foods occurring naturally around them, and in doing so they created a wide range of new crops, which, in the right climatic conditions, provided them with surpluses. Excess food enabled the population to expand and freed many people from the constant quest for nourishment, even allowing some to spend their time in the pursuit of knowledge and the arts and crafts.

One of the best examples of cultures flourishing in a sympathetic environment is that offered by the lush bottomlands of the Mississippi River, which provided abundant natural resources and rich soils for growing maize, beans, and squash. The largest center of the Mississippian archaeological tradition (see pages 32–33) was the city of Cahokia, which reached its cultural peak between 1050CE and 1250CE, when it supported as many as 35,000 residents. Cahokia's layout reflected sacred geometry, being dominated by a plaza surrounded by the giant Monk's Mound and sixteen other platform mounds. Monk's Mound, which was once crowned by a temple, is the largest prehistoric structure in the United States, with four platforms rising 100 feet (30 meters) from a base that is 1,040 feet (316 meters) long by 920 feet (241 meters) wide.

Cahokia symbolizes a major shift from nomadic to settled cultures and from populations that were relatively small to ones that were large and needed to be organized more like a state. No doubt people always have observed nature for clues about the weather, but as cities like Cahokia became more dependent on agriculture to sustain the lives of thousands, it became desirable to be able to predict growing

RIGHT **Big Horn Medicine Wheel on Medicine Mountain, Wyoming, is thought to be thousands of years old and explanations of its significance are many and varied. That there are dozens of similar wheels across North America stresses the widespread symbolic meanings of continuity, renewal, and infinity that are conferred upon the design.**

seasons. Cahokia's priests did this by building a woodhenge to mark the solstices and other key celestial events. A tall center pole and shorter poles around the outside circle marked the current position of the seasonal cycle.

It must be borne in mind that these new cultures essentially echoed the existing, age-old Native North American concern with the cycles of time, the seasons,

and life itself—a preoccupation of many historic cultures. The structure of Cahokia's woodhenge is not dissimilar to that of the ancient medicine wheel (see pages 49 and 92), which consists of a circle with a cross through it. As utilized by the Lakota people, the wheel's design is simplicity itself on one level, but on another it contains a whole cosmology. The quadrants created by the cross are red, black, white, and yellow—the sacred colors of humanity. The medicine wheel symbolizes a universe that is much more complicated than non-Indians might imagine.

The circle signifies the cyclical nature of all creation, while the cross marks the four cardinal directions from which the four winds blow. The cross also represents the four seasons recognized by the Lakota, which implies a temporal feature that gives the circle a "vertical" dimension. One way to look at this is to think of the cosmos as a sphere which contains every material element and event that happens. Because all events have been, are, or will be contained inside the sphere, they become timeless, although linked to a spatial element. The cross has not only a horizontal dimension through the center of the circle, but also a vertical dimension via a center pole. Things can be placed on layers within this space and everything can be connected. This connectedness constitutes a sacred quality.

The medicine wheel's pattern of the circle and the cross is highly visible in Indian culture—numerous dwellings and ritual structures mirror its cosmology almost exactly. For example, the lodges of the Pawnee, Arikara, and others replicated this round, celestial structure. Built out of cottonwood trees and earth, the spacious lodges had a hemispherical dome, usually supported by four central poles, and a hearth in the center with a smoke hole above it. The interior of these lodges (see illustration, opposite) is often divided into segments based on the cardinal directions and specific activities take place in those delineated areas. In similar vein, many of the more thoroughly nomadic Plains tribes, who erected circular *tipi*s to

LEFT  **The carefully restored interior of a Pawnee lodge. The painted buffalo skulls are facing east, where the tunnel-like entranceway is located. The central smoke hole can be seen above four poles representing the cardinal directions (see main text, right). The hole is large enough to afford a glimpse of the starry vault above, which the Pawnee believed had been created by Tirawahat.**

shelter in their encampments (see illustration page 38), build a temporary circular lodge for one of their most sacred renewal rituals, the Sun Dance. In the center of the lodge stands a tree or a center pole, from which hangs a buffalo skull that is carefully aligned with the eastern sun. Twelve smaller poles stand around the perimeter, indicating the orbiting movement of the Earth and a 12-moon year.

The cardinal directions are also an important feature of other Native American domestic structures, including the rectangular Haida plank houses built throughout the Northwest Coast region (see pages 18–19). Each of these dwellings represents the center of the universe for the kinship group that resides there. The houses stand on the shore facing the sea, with their entranceways flanked by towering carved totem poles; the back of the building looks to the forest (where the remains of the dead lie in wooden grave houses). The smoke from the hearth escapes skyward via a central smoke hole. Women utilize the left side of the house and men the right. The front of the building is for low-ranking people, while the rear is a place of power that is used ceremonially by the house chief. The vertical directions, up and down, are also crucial. The Haida believe in three worlds: an underworld, the world on which people live, and a sky world—during some ceremonies, a cedar sky pole is raised through the smoke hole to be climbed by a shaman drawing upon his sky powers.

Native people, then, are adapted in intimate ways to their landscapes, but their outlook is one of timelessness—they do not see the world in terms of linear sequences of cause and effect, nor in a temporal framework that has a beginning and an end. Extraordinary events are always tied to place, and with them comes a constellation of symbols that transcends normal temporal dimensions. Such events have creative force, and so do their symbols, which are timeless. Although the human actors may change, the fundamental principles of events never do: the sun always moves in the same direction; the stars always rise in the same pattern; people are

born and die. Events take on the character of immutable natural laws that are eternal realities of life in the passage from day to day, season to season. Time needs to be renewed through rituals that complete the cycle. This does not mean that Native North Americans do not understand or ever use chronological or calendrical time—of course, they do—only that life's most important events are simply not connected to that way of thinking.

Throughout Native North America the seasonal round of activities for daily life and ritual follows the pattern of the natural cycle—and nowhere is this better demonstrated than among the Pueblo peoples of the Southwest. Zuni life is oriented around events that are synchronized with the agricultural cycles, from summer solstice to winter solstice and back. The word for solstice, *itiwana*, means middle or center, a name the Zuni also apply to their village, the center of the world.

LEFT **Women performing in a feast-day corn dance at the Tewa pueblo of Santa Clara, New Mexico. Such communal events are part of the endless cycle that links the ceremonial and seasonal round of both ritual and agricultural life.**

## CAIRNS OF THE ARCTIC GIANTS

**Even the frozen lands of the far north provided rewards for resourceful hunters. Some Inuit developed the expertise to mount communal hunts of the migratory caribou that were central to their cultural and spiritual life, as reflected in the decoration of everyday objects (above). Stone cairns, called *inukshuk*s (opposite) and meant to resemble giant humans, are placed across the herds' main migratory routes, which drives them into places where hunters can ambush them. *Inukshuk*s are also used to navigate, signal where food is cached, and mark sacred ground.**

# CEREMONIAL CHAMBERS

LEFT An exposed *kiva* at Pueblo Bonito, New Mexico, built by the Anasazi (see page 58). This settlement grew after the community decided to settle rather than continue a semi-nomadic lifestyle. Gatherings were held in circular *kiva*s such as this, dug into the ground and normally covered. In Hopi *kiva*s today, prayers are sent to the underworld through the *sipapu*, the hole in the floor that is symbolic of the opening used during the primeval emergence (see pages 41–42).

Important rituals are often held in lodges or chambers built specially for the ceremonial event. Partly this is because of the numbers of people who participate, but more importantly it is to create a symbolic link to the sacred.

Rather than being permanent, the ritual structures of hunting and gathering peoples are often lightweight and intended to be easily transportable. For example, the Lakota sweat lodge—used for the *inipi* purification ceremony—is usually a simple frame of saplings bent into a small dome and covered with hides, tarps, or blankets. A pit in the center contains the heated rocks over which water is poured to produce steam. The Ojibwe build a special divination lodge, or "shaking tent," in which they call upon sacred beings for guidance. The tent consists of a barrel-like framework of poles about 7 feet (2 meters) tall, covered with birch bark, skin, or canvas. When the spirits respond to a conjurer's call, the wind that embodies them shakes the tent, and spirit voices can be heard talking or singing.

Groups of Plains Indians often hold all-night services of the Native American Church (a blend of Christian and traditional religious forms) in a special *tipi* that is larger than traditional residential *tipi*s, and covered with plain canvas. More permanent were the Mandan village farmers' ceremonial earth lodges, similar to those of the Pawnee (see page 51) and built near the center of the village. During their *okeepa* renewal ceremony, some participants sought visions by suspending themselves from the smoke hole of the lodge by means of thongs attached to piercings in their backs or chests.

But the best known of all Native North American ceremonial chambers is the *kiva* of the Hopi peoples of the Southwest, accessed from above by descending a ladder into its darkness. A feature of Pueblo architecture for at least a millennium (see illustration, opposite), the *kiva* hosts the *kachina* (spirit beings) ceremonies that are held from February until July to ensure that the universe continues to function harmoniously.

## MAGNIFICENT DWELLINGS OF THE ANCIENT ONES

Cliff Palace contains 151 rooms and 23 *kiva*s and is
one of nearly 600 native cliff dwellings in Mesa Verde
National Park in the Southwest. The cliff dwellings
were built by the Anasazi people, known as the
"Ancient Ones." The Anasazi were originally high-
country hunters and gatherers who lived in pit houses
that their ancestors had developed. Then in about
500CE the Anasazi people moved to the tops of mesas,
where they practiced dry-land farming. Although
the Anasazi had always used some of the natural cliff
alcoves, they started building residences in them only
around 1150CE.

By 1200CE most Anasazi were living in the cliffs.
Cliff dwellings were a major architectural
undertaking. People engineered their residences
and ceremonial structures to fit the contours of
the alcoves, carrying building stones from the canyon
slopes, along with dirt and water for mortar. Why the
Anasazi moved to the cliffs is unclear, although it may
be that some groups were fleeing internal conflicts.
Alternatively, the increasingly cold and dry climate
may have forced people to seek better shelter. Use of
the cliffs was short-lived—the Anasazi had migrated
further south by 1300CE, where they developed into
the Puebloan Hopi and Zuni peoples we know today.

# THE LIVING SPIRIT

Native North Americans believe that the creator endowed all things, living and non-living, with a spirit. In sharing this attribute, everything animate and inanimate is related and sacred; people are therefore expected to respect all things on Mother Earth. Indians understand that they are equals with plants and animals—in fact, as a result of links forged in the distant past, people are often kin to flora and fauna. The relationships between people, animals, plants, and the land are carefully explained in an extensive lore, and the rituals and ceremonies that form a core part of native life underline the links between the world that people inhabit and the realm of the spirits.

BELOW A war-pony effigy carved by a Plains Indian warrior. The holes marked in red paint indicate bleeding bullet wounds and probably mean that this horse was being honored after its death in battle. A warrior might emphasize his oneness with a mount by giving it the same protective paint patterns that he put on his own body before battle, confirming the spiritual bond that united man and beast.

# SPIRITS OF NATURE

Although there are many differences between native tribes, it is recognized by all groups that nature is imbued with spiritual significance. It is a realm where the worlds of humans and the spirits intersect, although the relationship between them can be complex. The spirits essentially maintain the world and reveal themselves in the form of natural phenomena, such as weather, wind, lakes, plants, and animals. These spirits are regarded as kin, and as such they have certain rights and obligations to each other as well as to the humans in whose proximity they live. Among some peoples, the power that controls the world is a more formless, mystical energy, such as Wakan among the Lakota and other Siouan-speaking peoples of the Plains, the Manitou of the peoples in the Great Lakes and Sub-Arctic regions, and Sila of the Baffin Bay Inuit.

Not only do plants, animals, and landforms have a spirit, they can actually *be* the spirit. An eagle is an eagle, but it can also be a thunderbird with special powers for protection; coyote is a coyote, but it can also be a manifestation of Trickster, willing to lead a human or other animal astray or to teach them a lesson. It is imperative for people, who have to live alongside these spirits, to know this and behave accordingly. If one obeys certain rules, there may be benefits; if one doesn't, there may be dire consequences. This concern with the spirits of nature does not in any way mean that

BELOW An Inuit ivory-carved walrus effigy pipe. Across the Arctic region it was believed that animals possessed a soul (*inua*) and that good craftsmanship would please the souls of prey—in return for respect being shown to them, animals would allow themselves to be caught.

either the spirit or nature is worshiped—not in the sense that the word conveys in Western religions. Rather, nature is revered at the same time that one lives with and uses it. Each group has its own ways of dealing with these invisible powers.

Elders teach children about nature spirits and how to deal with them, in the hope of ensuring a proper respect. Some individuals seek to harness and direct the power, or "medicine"—normally, this is attempted in a modest way, perhaps by using a talisman in a medicine bag or a bundle (see pages 72–73 and 78–79). Others might become specialists called holy people, medicine people, shamans, witches, or one of a range of other terms depending on how they use their power and skills (see pages 114–115).

Many activities are not intended to involve an individual dealing with the spirits, but are instead group obligations. Clans may be responsible for the maintenance of sacred medicine bundles that an ancestor or totemic being entrusted to the eternal care of descendants. A whole tribe may be responsible for performing ceremonies that ensure the annual renewal of the world. Good and evil may be determined by whether obligations to the spirits are met, which makes people careful to show respect at all times. Everyone must pay some level of attention to the spirits or the world becomes unbal-anced and threatens people's survival.

BELOW This conical Nootka woman's fiber hat is a distinctive type of headwear and bears a design of whale-hunts in progress. Along the Northwest Coast, the only peoples to specialize in this activity were the Nootka and their relatives the Makah, for whom whales were significant spirits as well as a food source.

**MASKS OF TRANSFORMATION**

The relationship between the sky, sea, humans, and spirits is a complex one. Among the Kwakiutl people of the Northwest Coast, masked dancers perform ceremonies that demonstrate beings transforming into other beings. The exquisitely carved masks change, as if by magic, into something different in response to the dancer pulling strings attached to the object's moving parts. It is said that the dancer can feel the spirits, who are believed to be carved into what he wears. This three-stage mask (above, left to right) shows a bull seal becoming first a sea raven and then a man, while this two-stage mask (opposite) is Raven becoming Raven of the Sea, accompanied by sharp-toothed creatures (facing inward).

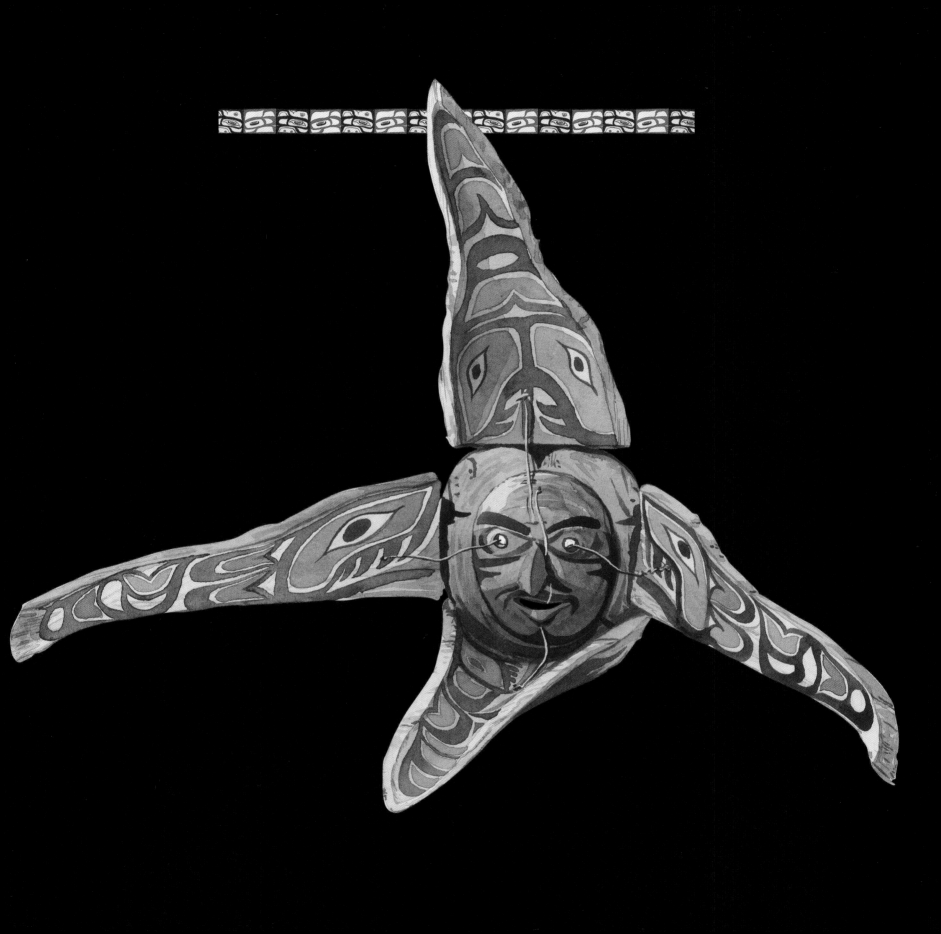

# ANCESTRAL ANIMALS

Relationships between Native North Americans and animals are profound and complicated. Many origin stories describe animals as being as old as the Earth itself; these animals then helped to create people and teach them how to live on the Earth, in touch with the mysteries of the natural world. However, over time, people grew proud and forgot many of these lessons, and this threw up barriers between humans and animals. Nevertheless, animals are still kin to humans and many groups continue to affirm that special relationship.

American Indians regard animals as both their sustenance and their closest living connection to creation, and they are observed carefully in an attempt to relearn the secrets of the natural world. People understand that animals give their own flesh so that humans can survive, and this debt is recognized by showing great respect.

Distinctions are sometimes made between the animals of today and those of the primordial time before the present creation, an age when beings could transform themselves from animal to human and back. Rarely, though, do tribes state that they are actually descended from animals; more commonly it is believed that some humans and animals share the same transformative being as an ancestor. At the time of creation, these beings lost the ability to transform, and the animals that now exist have never regained the power. For example, the Haida people in British Columbia say that bears walk upright and use their paws as hands to reveal their relationship to humans, with whom they could once talk and mate.

RIGHT **A gourd rattle incised and painted with a buffalo representation. Ceremonial songs performed during animal-honoring rituals are usually accompanied by such instruments. They are used to create the characteristic sounds associated with the animal spirits that the participants hope to invoke and make contact with during the ritual.**

The characteristic powers of particular animals can be of benefit to people. The Crow believe the elk to have special amorous powers, which is why in courting rituals men woo women by imitating elk sounds played on a long flute—a gift from Elk Man, who also presented the Crow with songs and a painted elk robe. Young suitors put on a robe, walk in front of the girl they love, and sing Elk Man's songs.

For many Plains groups, animal symbols are a central feature of many dances. Participants may wear: weasel hides to invest themselves with some of that animal's endurance; rabbit pelts to represent the humility each dancer must have in order to enter the center of the world in the middle of the dance circle; eagle feathers and eagle-bone whistles to honor the eagle's swiftness, courage, and strength, as well as its ability to communicate with both the Earth and the sky; a bear's skin to honor the great animal and persuade it to offer itself to hunters; or a buffalo skull to which grass is "fed" in an act that symbolizes the circle of life by nourishing the creature that sustains the people.

LEFT A colored engraving by George Catlin (1794–1872), ca. 1835, depicts a Bear Dance among the Siouan-speaking peoples of the Plains, who liked bear meat and used bear grease to oil their bodies. Led by a shaman clad in a full bearskin, the dancers sought to imitate and thereby honor their potential prey, thus encouraging the bear to sacrifice itself to the next group of hunters.

## AS SWIFT AS "SKY DOGS"

When the Blackfoot of the northern Plains first saw horses, they did not understand what they were: the strange creatures seemed like dogs, but were larger and swifter. The Blackfoot decided that Old Man, the creator, must have sent these creatures from the sky as a gift. Dogs had long been companions to humans, helping in the hunt and transportation; but those small animals could not match the phenomenal capabilities of the larger "sky dogs," which could carry a grown man, pull a transport of *tipi* poles loaded with possessions, and run as fast as the buffalo. The Lakota chose to call them *shunka wakan*, or "holy dogs," reflecting the seemingly supernatural potency that a horse's physical power exuded.

The Spanish had first introduced horses to the Southwest, after which the animal had later spread rapidly across the continent and changed the lives of all the native peoples that acquired them—especially on the vast, open Plains. Tribes that had hunted buffalo communally on foot shifted to fast-paced outings conducted by individuals on horseback, which enabled a good hunter to kill a number of animals quickly.

Among many Indian tribes, horses became an important measure of wealth and status. The Crow were renowned for their quantity of horses, while the horsemen of the Comanche and Cheyenne gained a formidable reputation for their riding abilities. A man's skill at handling his mount gave him considerable standing in his community, and the younger generation today has proudly tried to maintain this aspect of tribal culture. This Crow man, riding bareback with little equipment, is exhibiting his horsemanship at Hardin, Montana.

# TOTEM AND CLAN

Although most tribes believe that animals and people are closely related (see pages 66–67), only a few see themselves as the direct descendants of an animal spirit or totem, a word that derives from the Ojibwe *odem*, or "village." Tribal clans—that is, kinship groups or extended families—have stories about how they came to have a totem animal. The Hopi say that after their emergence (see pages 41–42), they decided to play a name game while they hunted and moved across the land in bands of relatives. Because the first band came across a bear skeleton, it decided to be called Bear Clan; another found a nest of spiders and became Spider Clan. Among other peoples, the origin may be even more direct: certain animals came back after their death (whether they had died of natural causes or given their lives to a human hunter), stripped off their animal fur or feathers to look and act like humans, and then established their own clan or village among the people.

The relationships within and between clans might reflect those that are thought to exist between their real-life animal namesakes, implying that clan members share its characteristics. For example, in the past, the Winnebago usually chose chiefs from the Thunderbird Clan, but it was members of the Bear Clan who policed the community, because bears are vigilant and all-seeing. Among the Cherokee, members of the Bird Clan acted as messengers, those of the Deer Clan served as runners, and men from the Wolf Clan fought as warriors.

A great deal of Native North American ritual and art is in imitation of totem animals, and representations of a clan animal are revered as a source of power. Help might be sought from an animal spirit by putting an emblem or fetish of the animal's power on a tool or weapon, or on their person. The Inuit engraved images of wolves on harpoons to evoke the wolf's predatory abilities, while the Crow covered their arrows with rattlesnake skin to allow them to strike swiftly.

RIGHT A Chilkat design is an abstract one based on clan totem animals. The design was a feature of mountain goat hair blankets, shirts, and ritual aprons among the Tsimshian, Tlingit, and some other peoples of the Northwest Coast. This Tlingit shirt features front and profile depictions of the bear, recognizable at the bottom from the rounded ears that appear above the lowest set of eyes.

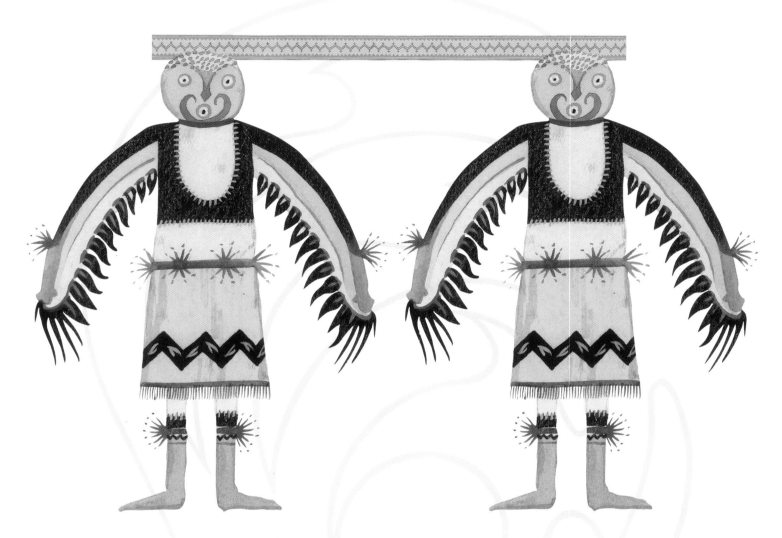

**RAPTOR MESSENGER OF THE SKY SPIRITS**

Birds can be portents of good or ill. Although all birds are honored, raptors are accorded particular respect, with eagles the most revered of all. Soaring high in the sky, many peoples associate the eagle with the sky gods and the weather. Seasonal rituals featuring eagle dancers (above) are one way that homage is paid. The eagle's swiftness, endurance, keen eyesight, and ferocity as a hunter made it an obvious icon of the warrior—eagle feathers symbolized achievements in battle, while body parts of an eagle (opposite) might form part of a medicine bundle or be used to adorn a *tipi* and bestow spiritual power on its owner.

# HEROES, TRICKSTERS, AND MONSTERS

The creators of the world were often vaguely human-like—and apparently part animal, but with god-like powers. Following creation, more familiar creatures came to inhabit the land and to render it more easily understood to humans. These imposers of order on an otherwise chaotic world are known as culture heroes—creative creatures who can transform their surroundings and themselves, while assuming human or animal characteristics and personalities in the process. Their counterparts are the trickster figures, who are also transformers. The trickster figures' activities often induce chaos and their energies are frequently directed into mischief-making. A trickster is an unpredictable force, but one that generally

teaches humans about their own foibles. One popular activity for culture heroes is the vanquishing of ferocious monsters that roam the Earth, creatures embodying the forces of evil and death.

These stories about heroes, tricksters, and monsters provide an allegorical form of explanation for how the world works. Trickster stories are especially important because they contain lessons about proper behavior and respect. Heroes exemplify intelligence, generosity, and sacrifices made for the good of the group. Preserved in their basic structure through lengthy oral tradition, the stories are often adjusted to meet the needs of each generation. Heroes come in many forms and include the often extraordinary activities of otherwise normal people. A hero might have been involved in the creation of human beings, have played a part in bringing new technology or beliefs to a group, or in saving the people from catastrophe. The Kiowa trickster-hero Saynday brought the sun from the other side of the world. Sweet Medicine gave the Cheyenne sacred arrows and the buffalo hat. Lone Man saved the Mandan from a great flood and established the tradition of leaving a plaza in the center of the village in which to dance.

The actions of culture heroes can change the course of a tribe's history. White Buffalo Calf Woman brought the Lakota an important gift at a time when the people were hungry. Two young men went to look for buffalo, but had no luck. As they hunted, a woman dressed entirely in white buffalo skin came toward them—one hunter realized she was a holy person and filled his mind with good thoughts; the other saw her only as a beautiful woman and reached out to take her. A cloud covered them, and when it cleared there was nothing left of the second man except his skeleton. The woman gave the good hunter a message: she would bring the Lakota a sacred object in four days' time. On her return, she brought a pipe of red stone, which she told them represented the Buffalo People's flesh and blood as well as that

LEFT **A buffalo emerges from a wintry mist in Yellowstone National Park, Wyoming. A characteristic of tribal mythology is the way it intertwines everyday creatures on whom the people depended for survival. Ancient Lakota stories explain how their links with the buffalo were forged (see main text, right).**

of all other people. The pipe stem represented all the plants growing on the Earth. The smoke passing through the pipe and stem represented the sacred wind that carries prayers to the creator, Wakan Tanka. She demonstrated how to present the pipe to the Earth, the sky, and the four sacred directions. When she left, she turned into a white buffalo calf. Adult buffalo then came to the village so that people could hunt them, and the Lakota have prayed with the Sacred Pipe ever since.

Unlike heroes, tricksters tend to be unpredictable, selfish, and rascally, and they almost always have some exaggerated human characteristics. A trickster's reckless behavior brings change, but he usually has a humorous side. The trickster dupes others, but is always duped himself in the end. He has few morals or values and no control over his desires. Almost any animal can be a trickster. Coyote is a favorite trickster for many Indian nations (see page 90); the Apache believe Coyote can talk, dress, and act like a human, but often runs around on four legs. Some Northwest Coast tribes had Mink, who was always getting into trouble as a result of his voracious sexual appetite. Other Northwest Coast and Sub-Arctic groups had Raven, who was especially helpful when he worked his wiles on other supernatural beings. The Tsimshian form of Raven is a master changeling, who wears Raven clothing that he can take off to reveal his man-form. A number of other tricksters, such as the Ojibwe's Nanabush (see illustration, opposite), can do something similar— Nanabush is half man and half spirit, who can appear disguised as an ordinary man, although he possesses the powers of a shaman. He is well-meaning, but often gives in to his baser whims.

Monsters are genuinely evil and seek to wreak disruption, harm, and death wherever they go. For example, the Abenaki fear the Chenoo. Much like the Windigo of many Great Lakes tribes, the Cheeno is a powerful cannibal who was once a

human being, but was turned into a monster because of his greed and hunger. Almost impossible to kill, he roams the land, seeking people to consume. The Kwakiutl had a shark-like spirit called Yagim; it followed canoes, which it sometimes capsized, eating the displaced humans as they struggled in the waves. When vindictive, Yagim could send raging storms and huge waves, which might destroy a village.

**LEFT** **This painting by Blake Debassige, entitled** *The Great and Mischievous Nanabush,* **features the creator-trickster figure well known among the Ojibwe people. His magical origins enabled him to transform into anything. He is depicted here as a giant crossing the Great Lakes, carrying fish to eat and using the islands as stepping stones.**

## DIVINE PROTECTION AND POWER

In a universe filled with uncertainty, Native North Americans, like other peoples, seek assurances of protection and success. For some, these might arise in a dream or vision with the revealing of a special emblem to be painted on an object, such as this shield showing a she-bear protecting her young (right). Others believe that careful observation of the world will reveal special knowledge by means of which humans will attain some control over their destiny. This is the reasoning behind objects of power such as palm-sized fetishes, to be held in the hand. The Zuni people, among others, carve these in the form of ancestral animals and call upon their spirits for protection and healing, as well as many other benefits (above, clockwise from the bottom left, are badger, guardian of the south; frog, for bringing rain; snake, for hunting dangerous animals; and mountain lion, protector from surprise attack).

# DREAM VOYAGES

The people of many Indian tribes regard dreams—which provide a personal connection to the spirit world—as an extension of daily life. Unlike visions, which are often sought after and need to be induced (see pages 118–119), dreams come unbidden when one is asleep and the soul is roaming free of the body. Dreams might relate to an individual or involve matters that concern the whole tribe. They can be a source of great spiritual power, imparting wisdom or even foretelling the future.

LEFT **"Dreamcatchers" sway in the breeze in Monument Valley. Although these items originated much further north among the Ojibwe, some Navajo say that Spider Woman's spinning activities inspired them (see pages 100-101). Dreamcatchers are usually hung over a bed—their web filters out bad dreams, while the small hole in the center allows only good thoughts to enter the sleeper's mind.**

In a dream, a person may learn a song that must be sung during rituals or in times of danger or stress; he or she may be warned to avoid certain foods or activities. Dreams can be a defense against evil by giving warning of an attack by witches or by providing information about a means of protection. Many groups emphasize the power that can be transmitted through dreams. For the Washo of the Great Basin region, a man who dreams of rabbits or antelopes might become a skilled hunter. The first signs that a Washo is to be invested with shamanic power also comes in a series of dreams, which usually feature an animal such as an owl or bear. The Washo do not seek to become shamans, and such dreams are often unwelcome. Most dreamers initially refuse shamanic power, but when they finally accept it their dreams become instruction sessions in curing or divination, received from a *wegaleyo*, or spirit being.

The Huron of the Northeastern Woodlands believed that there was little difference between the world of daily life and that of dreams. The soul had intense hidden desires that were often revealed in dreams, which were said to be the language of the soul. Dreams were seen as real, because during sleep the soul was thought to leave the body and travel to the place where what was being dreamed about actually existed. The dreamer might be given information, instructions, messages, or even be shown the future. If the dreamer failed to heed the dream, the soul became angry and caused illness and misfortune. As a result, the Huron paid particular attention to any dreams that occurred just before they went hunting, fishing, trading, or to war. So much did they rely on dreams for guidance in everyday life that the first Jesuit priests to contact the Huron described dreams as the tribespeople's main god. Sometimes advice received in dreams was followed in preference to advice given by the tribal chiefs. However, not all dreams were assumed to be reliable—public confidence in an individual's dream varied according to his or her social status and how many of that person's earlier dream predictions had come true.

# SACRED SOCIETIES

Centered on holy beings, objects, rituals, or ideals, Native North American sacred societies often cut across kinship structures. A person's social identity, and sometimes even their personality traits, derived from society membership. The entire culture viewed the duties of each sacred society as crucial to the survival of the whole, because their efforts kept the world in balance.

The constitution and duties of a sacred society could be as variable as the tasks performed. If the society was age-based, this provided useful ways of allocating both sacred and civic obligations. Societies could also be used to educate youth and provide social control. The Eastern Cherokee linked their political activities to the round of major religious ceremonies: the tribal officials belonging to the White Peace Organization Chiefs conducted criminal courts and religious tribunals, controlled marriage and divorce, and trained boys to hunt. They also ran the ritual cycle of several maize ceremonies and the Reconciliation, New Moon, and Bounding Bush ceremonies. Among the Iroquois, members of the False Face Society (see illustration, right) played an important role as healers who could sing away sickness.

A sacred society's power derived from the spirit world, sometimes through direct links. A False Face healer's mask was common in form, but individually it possessed distinctive features derived from the wearer's dreams and imagination. This interaction with other forces is found throughout Native North America—at certain Mandan rituals, spiritual beings actually participated in ceremonies through human impersonators; similarly, at some Kwakiutl initiation ceremonies spirits might participate through puppets. The rituals a society performed were often acts to obtain divine blessings for the tribe: for example, members of the Cherokee Booger Society dance to maintain the precarious harmony of the Cherokee people with their environment.

RIGHT **Dressed as a member of the False Face Society, a man poses in front of a reconstructed Iroquois birchbark longhouse. His mask has the distinctive crooked nose of the legendary giant who challenged the Creator to a contest of strength and lost. Members of the False Face Society were curers who used ashes and tobacco to perform a ritual, at the same time shaking turtleshell rattles to drive away the cause of the patient's illness.**

## WHERE *MANITOU*S DWELL

For the peoples of the Eastern Woodlands and Great Lakes, powerful forces of nature called *manitou*s were present everywhere. They ranged in character from those that were benevolent to others that were life-threateningly malicious. People learned about the *manitou*s at an early age, and through the teachings of elders and their own dreams they came to understand the many powers of the spirits.

Even so, such beliefs made the region's vast areas of thick forest potentially perilous places that reverberated with mystery—and the woodland could hardly be avoided because it was so rich in plant and animal life that its produce could sustain a people throughout the year.

The most remote *manitou*s were celestial and lived high in the sky, while some lived just below them as the spirits of the birds. Many *manitou*s, including some of the worst, lived in the area's many lakes and streams. The earthly ones often resided in odd features of the landscape such as this rocky outcrop in New York State's Shawangunk Mountains, which overlooks thick forest. Those *manitou*s who lived in the forbidding darkness under the canopy of trees were in charge of the animals, and could thus either help or impede hunters. Dangers also lurked in the form of the evil *manitou*s such as Windigo, the cannibal monster who lay in hiding to await the unwary traveler.

# EVEN THE SACRED CHANGES

Gradual syncretism—the process of blending or hybridization that occurs between religious beliefs when cultures come together—was part of Native North American life in pre-Contact times, as demonstrated in the slow spread of the Sun Dance complex across the Plains. However, when the settlers brought Christianity, syncretism became abrupt and inevitable. Christian missionaries went to great lengths to change Indian behavior and beliefs, forcing children to learn Christian practice, and outlawing certain native ceremonies, such as the flesh offerings of the Sun Dance among the Lakota.

Some missionaries did recognize that the native concept of a "great spirit" was similar to that of the Christian God, and tried to translate one belief system into another. In the Handsome Lake Movement found among the Seneca of the Iroquois Confederation in the late 1700s, a combination of traditional beliefs with Quaker practice helped to relieve the Seneca of some of the pressure to assimilate to European ways. In the messianic Ghost Dance movement that took hold among some Plains and Plateau groups, Christian imagery of the end of the world became entwined with tribal beliefs. The Native American Church began in the 1800s and had become widespread across the Great Plains by the mid-twentieth century. Its use of traditional local beliefs, Christian imagery, and the mildly hallucinogenic peyote cactus all came together in "peyote meetings." Often held overnight in a *tipi*, these services feature Christian objects, such as Bibles and crucifixes, but are filled with other elements that appeal specifically to a native audience.

LEFT **The silhouette of a braided Native North American man leaning near a church bell and cross in the New Mexico twilight. Spanish missionaries had significant influence in the Southwest in the 16th and 17th centuries. Today, many inhabitants of the Pueblos practice a syncretic blend of their native religion and Catholicism. For example, each Pueblo celebrates the feast day of its patron saint with performances of native ceremonial dancing.**

LEFT Dancers at New Mexico's San Ildefonso Pueblo wear typically elaborate headdresses and colorful robes to take part in the "Los Matachines," a dance drama that depicts the struggle between good and evil. Although Pueblo stories recount that the play originated in Mexico with the Aztec leader Montezuma, in fact it was probably based on the morality plays of medieval Spain brought to New Mexico by Spanish Franciscans in the 16th or 17th centuries.

# SYMBOL, MYTH, AND COSMOS

In spite of the rich variety of Native North American belief systems, the many First Peoples of this vast land share a great deal of sacred history and wisdom. From creation stories to the part played by natural cycles in influencing Indian world views, certain important themes recur. Interaction with the environment and all its life-forms, in the form of foodstuffs, raw materials, agriculture, hunting, and so on, has fundamentally shaped Indian life, domestic culture, artistic practices, and decorative techniques. The result is an interdependent, connected cosmos whose richness and variety are celebrated in order that things might continue to exist in their bountiful and harmonious cycle.

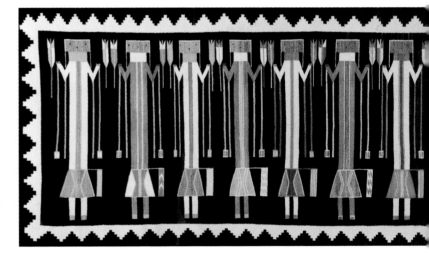

# EARTHDIVERS
# AND WORLD MAKERS

Native American mythology is a sacred form of history that contains many explanations for what people see around them every day. Filled with powerful metaphors and anthropomorphized animals, these tales feature sexual union, conflict, joy, hardship, respect, and the whole spectrum of human behavior and emotions as the narratives attempt to make sense of the beginning of the world.

Some tribes believe that the beginning was a featureless void, and the actions of gods brought the world into existence. For example, the Apaches believe that Black Wind made the Earth and Yellow Wind gave it light, while other spirits created life and the geographical features of the world. There are groups that believe the world had always existed, but that it lacked definition until a Creator or Great Spirit acted. For the Shasta this figure was Old Man Above, who climbed down through a hole in the sky to make the world. He brought Sun, which melted the world's snow and ice to form its waters. According to some tribes, the Earth underwent fundamental change due to the action of a hero or trickster (see pages 74–76), usually an animal. A tale from the Nez Percé is typical of this type of creation story and features Coyote, who can be both trickster and hero. After slaying a terrible monster, Coyote decided to celebrate by creating human beings. He scattered pieces of the monster's body, and in each spot where a piece of corpse landed, a tribe of Indians appeared. When his friend Fox pointed out that Coyote hadn't created a tribe at the place where he killed the monster, he was sad because he had no parts left. He cleverly wiped the blood from his hands and let it drip to the ground, declaring: "Here I make the Nez Percé; their numbers will be few, but they will be strong and pure."

Earthdiver myths constitute a common genre of creation story. In these tales, there is no dry land, only water, and a familiar animal is asked to dive under the

water to bring mud from the bottom—from which the world is then formed. The Arapaho tell how an old man, Flat Pipe, was tired of being in water all the time, so he begged some ducks for help. They dived to the bottom and a few brought up some mud in their bills, but it was not enough. Then Turtle swam by. Again, Flat Pipe asked for help. Happy to oblige, Turtle eventually brought up enough mud to satisfy Flat Pipe. That is how dry land came to be. The muskrat and beaver are also common Earthdivers because they use mud from the riverbed to build their lodges.

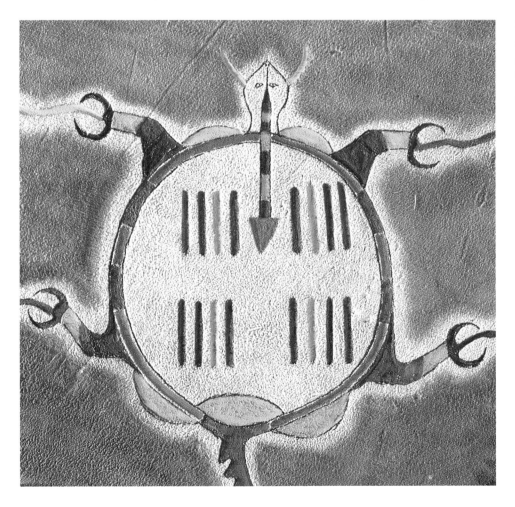

LEFT A Cheyenne buckskin shield decorated with a sacred turtle design. Turtles are common in Earthdiver tales—some Cheyenne say that the burden of the primeval mud carried around on Turtle's back is the reason that he moves so slowly. As a result, turtles often symbolize patience.

# CIRCLE OF TIME

The circle is omnipresent in Native North America and symbolizes "connected-ness," or the sacred unity of all things. Time itself is seen as circular (see pages 50–53), and the various cycles of nature are evidence of the eternal circle of existence. Each day follows a cyclical rhythm, with the sun rising above the horizon and then moving across the sky and slipping below the horizon again, to be replaced by the moon and stars. The heavens change, but with a marvelous regularity, which tribes on the Plains represent by creating medicine wheels that mirror the movement of the sun, moon, planets, and stars. These large circles of stones, often with spokes radiating from the center (see page 49), are thought to mark the solstices, the risings of important stars, and other celestial events.

Most tribes have a ceremonial cycle that reflects the endless repetition of the seasons—the new growth of spring, followed by the maturation of summer, the decline of autumn, and the death of winter (see page 53). Various groups devised their own methods of marking key seasonal changes. For example, the ancient Anasazi of the Southwest pecked spirals into rock faces. Archaeologists speculate that when shadows or light touched certain parts of the spiral, this indicated the optimum times to plant. The Hopi select a human "sun watcher," whose task is to observe the sun's movements each day and calculate when the last frost of the year will occur from the timing of the winter solstice. Some tribes of the Northwest use the spawning of salmon as a seasonal marker, just as some Southwest groups watch for the ripening of the saguaro cactus fruit. Among the Lakota, this observation extends to the naming of some months: for example, July is Cherry Ripening Moon. Certain animals—such as the snake, which regularly sloughs off its skin—are also associated with renewal.

Each person's life is similarly a cycle of birth, growth, maturation, death, and regeneration, punctuated by rites of passage. Native North Americans believe that nothing ever really ends. Instead, when living beings complete a cycle, they move to the past—remaining "out there," immanent and near by, rather than distant.

The importance of the circle of time is reflected in the many spirals and circles that appear in Native North American art and architecture. Even people's homes were often round, whether a Blackfoot hide-covered *tipi*, a Hidatsa earth lodge, or a Wichita grass-covered lodge. The circle is particularly prevalent in ritual life: in Mistassini Cree lodges on cold winter nights, hunters pass large hand drums around a circle to accompany personal songs of thanks to the animals that gave their lives for the people; at the Lakota *inpi*, or sweat-lodge ceremony, participants sit in a circular lodge, and during bouts of song and prayer, a small, circular hand drum is passed from person to person. Similarly, at a powwow, dancers enter the arena and move in a circuit around the dance floor. When each group of singers and their drum are called, they form a ring around a large, round drum raised slightly from the floor. Songs tend to be sequential in form, with a leader singing alone, followed by others in unison, punctuated regularly by three or four so-called "honor beats" on the drum.

Inter-tribal dances are usually "round dances" in which the dancers hold hands and move in a circle or spiral that gravitates toward the center and back. Similarly, in a dance that symbolizes renewal, hoop dancers may use one or many hoops, twirling them around their arms, legs, or neck as they dance to form shapes such as the sun, the moon, and thunderbirds.

LEFT **This Cahuilla coiled basket from California symbolizes, in its coiled, spiral form and its use of a rattlesnake design, the endless natural cycle of death and renewal. Many tribes in California associate the rattlesnake with longevity and renewal.**

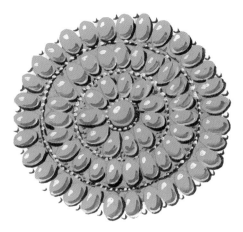

### THE UNIFYING CIRCLE

In the natural world, circles are a recurrent form—the life-giving sun is a disk,

while a pebble thrown into water creates circular ripples. The conceptual power

of the circle is strong in Native North America: it symbolizes balance, unity, and

renewal, and provides an artistic and symbolic motif that appears with regularity.

The most ancient rock art on the continent depicts circles—this prehistoric

Chumash rock painting (above) is the work of a ritual specialist—as does traditional

basketry and jewelry (above, left and right) and modern beadwork (opposite).

# THE HOLINESS
# OF ARTISTRY

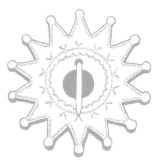

Traditional Native North American art serves a vital role for the people. As with all art, it reflects the society in which the artist resides, as well as his or her individual creativity. However, it encompasses more than that—for Indians, art represents the Earth and all its inhabitants by means of both the materials used and the rich religious symbolism that is inherent in each culture's history. Native North American art provides a means for people to connect to the sacred.

The inspiration for art is often a spiritual experience. For example, a dream might reveal to the artist a design for a warrior's shield or part of a dancer's regalia. The symbols and patterns that adorn many native objects are not seen as mere representations. A deer etched into the shoulder of a pot is thought actually to *be* a deer; a killer whale painted on a plank house is invested with the spirit of the killer whale; and a circle and cross can *be* the entire cosmos. Although all traditional Native North American art reflects the surrounding world and has religious significance, it also has a purely aesthetic significance. Finely made objects are considered worthy of praise and can be appreciated in their own right. The best artists and craftspeople are highly prized and they enjoy great social prestige.

Native art is remarkably diverse. A wealth of decorative motifs embellish objects made from every conceivable natural material. Fibers stripped from plants and trees are plaited into baskets; animal hair is spun and woven into patterned cloth and blankets; clay is turned into pottery and incised or painted; while stone, bone, and wood are exquisitely carved. Jewelry may include quillwork, beadwork, fur, metal, bone, and colorful stone, all used in an immense variety of ways. To some degree, the medium helps to determine the content and form of artistic designs. Geometric motifs are easiest to render in basketry, beading, and weaving, while

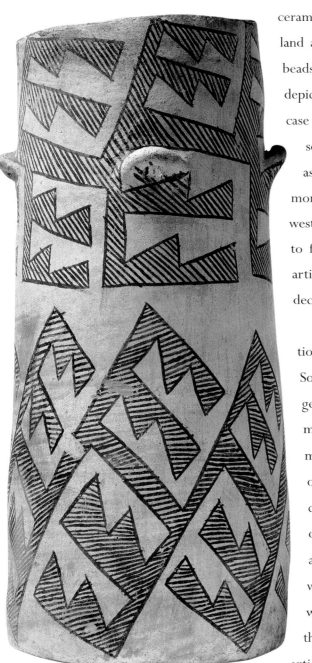

ceramics, carving, and painting allow greater naturalism. Woodland artists use moose hair, porcupine quills, and glass trade beads to execute wonderful floral forms. However, a realistic depiction of nature is not always the cultural norm, as in the case of the Northwest Coast tribes, for whom a stylized representation of an animal's key identifying characteristic, such as the dorsal fin on a killer whale or the beak of a raven, is more important than realism (see pages 18–19). In the Southwest, prehistoric Mimbres pottery used geometric decorations to frame stylized animal and human forms. Contemporary artists now use the old Mimbres motifs in many new ways to decorate a range of objects from pottery to tiles.

Indian artists mostly work according to established traditions, but are able to experiment within acceptable limits. Some cultures may limit or restrict artists based on clan, gender, age, or some other consideration. For example, members of a particular clan can be prohibited from using motifs owned by another clan, or from depicting the totem of their own clan. Women may not be allowed to work with certain materials that are considered ritually polluting or dangerous, such as the blood, fur, or bones of animals such as the bear. Men may be expected to work in some media while women work in others—a sexual division of labor which has sometimes changed over time. With pottery, in the Pueblos of the pre-Contact era men were usually the artisans, but now women often do such work and receive the

LEFT **This pitcher with a geometric pattern was made by the ancient Chaco Anasazi people. Today pottery in the Southwest still has a variety of distinctive black-on-white forms, continuing an age-old tradition begun by the Anasazi and the Mimbres cultures. Modern black-on-white pottery is most commonly found among the western Keresan-speaking Pueblos and their neighbors, the Zuni.**

most recognition for fine ceramics—which may be etched, painted, or burnished, and are executed in colors that range from browns and natural reds to creams, black, and white. In a region peopled by agriculturalists, pots and jars are made out of the Earth's most basic elements and they contain or process life-sustaining seeds and water. The craft strengthens the link between the culture and its environment.

This relationship can be seen in many places, with each culture area being known for particular art forms because the local environment provides specific raw materials and the inspiration for the embellishment. Along the Northwest Coast, with its abundant cedar forests, wood carvers create totem poles and masks that feature stylized representations of sea animals. Plains artists use hide, beads, feathers, and quillwork in amazing ways to represent bison, antelope, and other

BELOW **The diamond-and-trident symbols on this beadwork saddlebag identify it as originating among the Plains cultures. Geometric designs are often used in native art to symbolize sacred spirits or events.**

grassland creatures. Inuit carvers transform bone and ivory into realistic figurines of seals, polar bears, and other Arctic animals, as well as fanciful versions of mythological beings. Women of the Huron, Micmac, and other tribes of the densely wooded Northeast and Great Lakes used quills sourced from the abundant tree-dwelling porcupine to decorate utilitarian objects with floral patterns.

Although the Southwest is perhaps most famous for its pottery, weaving has been practiced there for millennia. Navajo women are particularly celebrated for their weaving skills (see pages 100–101). They learned the art from their Pueblo neighbors between 1500 and 1800 and have continually adapted it since, not only to meet demand, but also in keeping with the importance in Navajo philosophy of the concepts of change, transformation, and renewal.

Native North American crafts have always been highly adaptable—tribes traded new and exotic materials over vast distances for centuries before white people arrived. Then, as brightly colored trade beads became available after Contact, they replaced or were combined with quills in intricate patterns. Colors also changed as new dyes became available. On the Plains today, exquisite beadwork with traditional themes may be applied to an object such as a baseball cap. Meskwaki (Fox) men and women have become experts in appliqué, using shiny fabric to replace the floral patterns once made from quills or beads. These adaptations are typical of the ways in which native artistic traditions have expanded as new media, materials, and techniques have been borrowed from Euroamerican colonizers. Some scholars maintain that, with the production of non-traditional forms and themes, contemporary native art has lost its spiritual center—but Indian art is primarily spiritual and adaptations are the responses of artists to the new challenges that native people face in their lives.

ABOVE A classic Navajo "Chief's Blanket." Such handsome items, valued for the boldness and simplicity of their designs, were traded throughout the Southwest and Great Plains in the 19th century. Weaving is a sacred, highly valued activity for Navajo women, who believe that a mythic female ancestor, Spider Woman (see pages 100–101), wove the universe out of sacred materials in the cosmos.

## SPIDER WOMAN'S BLESSING

Spider Rock soars nearly 800 feet (245 meters) above Arizona's Canyon de Chelly, and in a cave atop the rock is said to reside Spider Woman, one of the most revered Navajo deities. Using her great supernatural powers, she once protected the Navajo as they emerged into the world. Her husband created a loom for her out of elements of the cosmos, and with this loom Spider Woman taught the people to weave.

Spider Woman appropriately provides a connection between Navajo mythology, the landscape, the divine gift of artistry, and everyday culture. Navajo children still believe that Spider Woman is kept informed by Talking God about those who misbehave, and that if they continue to be naughty they will be carried away to Spider Rock and eaten by her.

Historically, the Navajo were almost certainly taught the art of weaving by the Pueblo Indians, who had worked with cotton for generations. Navajo women began to practice in earnest during the 17th century, using wool from sheep imported by the Spanish, and today Navajo weavers have achieved international recognition.

In the early days of commercial weaving, women still left a small hole at the center of their work in honor of the spider's web, but as trade increased in importance the practice was replaced by a "spirit outlet" (a thin flaw from the center to the edge). The ability to weave remains an important part of female Navajo life and traditional culture advocates that young girls be prepared for their future by having a spider's web rubbed on their hands and arms.

# SPIRIT WORLDS

The realm of Native North American spirits reflects the realm of human beings. For most tribes, the domain of the spirits contains places, plants, and animals like those that surround people. The various spirit worlds are parallel universes, considered to be as real as the Earth, but often portrayed as rather formless—for example, a tribe may believe in a world "out there" of the future or past. Spirit worlds are most visible in creation stories, but can also be glimpsed in visions and in the symbolic structure of rituals. Certain individuals, known as shamans or holy people (see pages 114–117), are thought to have special powers that enable them to gain access to spirit realms. Among the Northwest Coast tribes and the Arctic and Sub-Arctic peoples, shaman-empowered dolls are thought to be directly in touch with the spirit world. Belief in these other realms is important, for without them the world of humans makes little sense.

The sky is peopled by many mythic figures and is seen as a parallel structure—and it is as such that it features in numerous Indian creation stories (see pages 40–43). "The sky comes down to Earth," as the Skidi Pawnee say. Sometimes the sky must be brought together with the Earth, wedded in sexual union. The Zuni believe that, at the beginning, Mother Earth and Father Sky lay together in the primordial waters (another world

RIGHT **A wooden Tanaina "shaman doll," from Cook Inlet in northwest Canada. Usually dressed as people, such dolls were generally believed to have a life of their own. Among the Yuguk of western Alaska, this type of doll is empowered by shamans, who place it in a tree at a secret location and consult it during the year. The doll uses its connection to the spirit world to tell the shamans where game can be found.**

mentioned in many creation stories). When she grew large with offspring, Mother Earth separated from Father Sky and slid beneath the waters. Once they are united, traffic between Earth and sky becomes possible, with figures such as the thunderbird having the ability to move between the worlds.

For the Lakota, the Black Hills and the nearby Badlands (see pages 40–41) form a mirror image of the spirit world. The Lakota believe that at one time there were no hills on the vast, uninterrupted Plains. This was a chaotic realm, where humans and animals preyed on one another. Humans changed this by summoning all the animals to take part in a race that followed a circular path outlined on the flat ground. The frenzied animals ran round and round the path so many times that the commotion caused by their pounding feet not only disturbed the spirits but also began to cause the path to sink into the Plains. The "racetrack" can still be seen encircling the hills. The ground within the circle rose up to form the mountains, which eventually burst with dust and rocks, killing many of the animals, including the Unkcheghila giants, whose large bones can still be found in the Badlands. Humans survived, thus earning the right to prey on the other animals. However, the hills—now called the "heart of everything that is"—remain to remind humans of their insignificance in comparison to the inhabitants of the spirit world.

Sometimes Native North Americans even build their homes to replicate or symbolize their people's cosmology. For example, an Ojibwe bark lodge is thought of as a sphere intersected by several planes. Half of the lodge cannot be seen, because it lies in the underworld. The half that people inhabit reflects what they see, because they live on the plane that bisects the sphere—that is, on the ground. But above them stretches the invisible life path that mirrors the heavens, and the eternal path people follow when they leave behind their existence on Earth and undertake their final journey to the spirit world (see pages 132–134).

# HUNTERS AND PREY

One of the central beliefs of Native North Americans is that animals understand that for people to survive and stay warm they must be eaten and their pelts worn. It is thought that in exchange for their sacrifice animals wish to be honored at all times and that they carefully observe how humans behave toward them. As a result, much ritual surrounds the special relationship between hunters and their prey.

The Mistassini Cree took great care to demonstrate their respect for animals. The most powerful spirits, such as that of Bear, had to be treated with particular consideration—when a bear was killed, his bones were placed on a platform in a tree so that dogs and other scavengers could not get to them. The Cree also honored smaller prey, such as beavers and rabbits, by tying the dead animals' skulls and feet into bundles, which they hung from trees. (These traditions also made ecological sense: the numbers of platforms or bundles allowed hunters to keep track of the quantity of animals taken and thus avoid overhunting their territory.)

Hunting rituals were performed in order to lure prey in times of need. On the Plains, whenever the buffalo were scarce tribes would attempt to call them by mounting a ritual, often in the form of a special dance. The Mandan would offer bowls of food to the head of a dead buffalo in the hope that a show of generosity would encourage other buffalo to give themselves to the hunters. Plains hunters from different tribes sang songs or displayed fetishes to lure buffalo. Pueblo Indians called deer by performing a ritual in which men wearing deer costumes would act like the prey and would then be symbolically "killed."

Individuals sometimes carried out additional rituals or followed practices that were based on special relationships or pledges made to a certain species. For example, a hunter might vow only to hunt during certain seasons, or to say a special prayer (perhaps revealed to him in a dream) while an animal was being killed.

RIGHT **This necklace, made out of grizzly-bear claws by Meskwaki (Fox) Indians on the fringes of the Plains and Great Lakes regions, would have been worn by a hunter as a mark of distinction. The right to wear such an object was a rare honor, won through a display of bravery when confronted with the much-respected Bear spirit.**

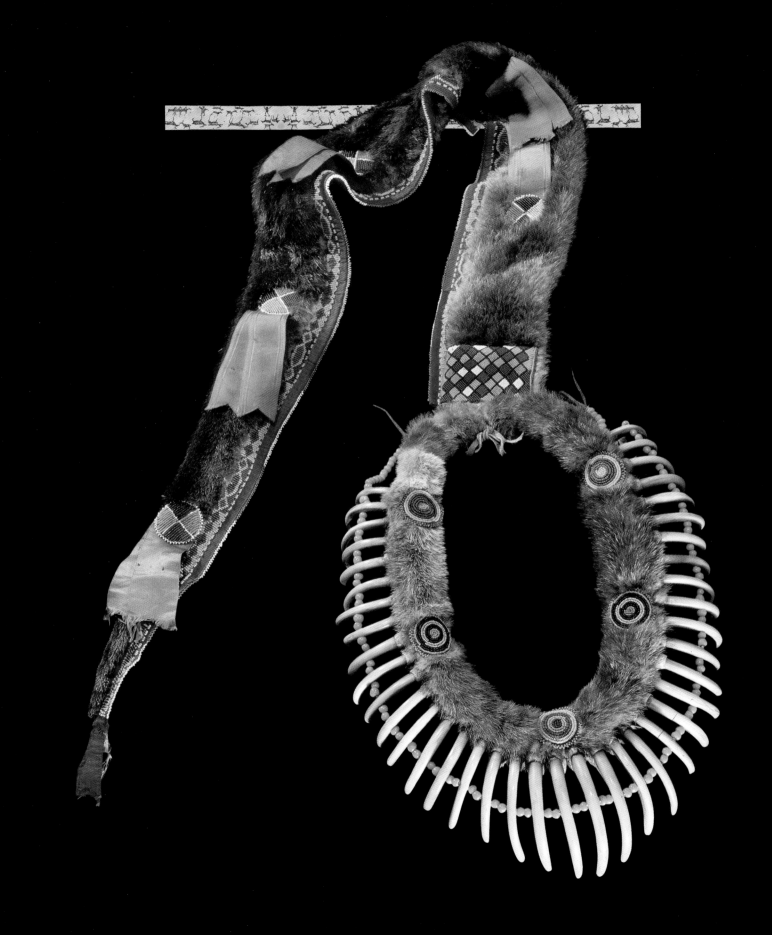

## RETURN OF THE BUFFALO NATION

"You, O buffalo, are the Earth! May we understand this!" goes a Lakota Sun Dance prayer, demonstrating in no uncertain terms the importance of *tatanka*, the Lakota word for buffalo. For many Plains tribes the American bison was the source of life. Buffalo were among the first animals hunted by the original inhabitants of the continent, and in their death they helped to sustain Indian nations for countless generations. In addition to meat, either fresh or in storable pemmican form, there was seemingly no limit to what *tatanka* yielded: hides could be made into robes and *tipi* covers; horns could be formed into spoons; the bladder could be used to carry water; and sinew could be used for bows.

On the vast grasslands of the Plains, tribes centered much of their culture on the huge, black-haired animal, which took its place as one of their most sacred spirits. Ceremonies revolved around the buffalo, from calling them to be hunted when times were hard to venerating them, through the figure of White Buffalo Calf Woman (see pages 75–76) and as part of renewal rituals such as the Sun Dance.

Herds of buffalo were once so enormous that the ground thundered underfoot as they moved through an area. But by the late 1880s commercial hunters had driven the buffalo close to extinction. The buffalo-based, nomadic Plains Indian lifestyle came to an end. However, both the Indians and the buffalo have survived. Many tribes now raise herds of the animals on their lands—like this group in Custer State Park in the Black Hills. It can be said that the Buffalo Nation has returned.

# GATHERING THE EARTH'S ABUNDANCE

**M**other Earth provided Indians with astounding gifts, even in seemingly difficult environments. Hunters could, of course, obtain game provided that they had sufficient skill and luck, but for most native peoples plants represented by far the most important source of food.

Gathered from the earliest times, edible seeds had high nutritional value and were a key resource in almost every region except the Arctic. Fruit and berries provided energy and flavor, while roots and greens were useful sources of carbohydrates and fiber. However, some wild plants required complex processing systems: for example, the Pomo of California managed to produce flour from acorns, but only after they had devised a system that used flowing water to leach out the high levels of tannic acid that the nuts contain. In the Great Lakes area, where wild rice grew in abundance, people would go out after the crop had matured and gather the rice by knocking the grains into their canoes. Back on land, they would parch the rice, pour it into purpose-built, lined pits and then don special moccasins that enabled them to stomp off the hulls of the grains.

By about 700BCE, Native North Americans in several regions had begun to modify plants such as sunflower, amaranth, and marsh elder, which grew naturally in areas of disturbed, nitrogen-rich soil near villages and along streams. Squashes and gourds were plentiful in the Eastern Woodlands and became early cultivated crops. The most important crop of all was maize (see pages 110–111), domesticated in Central America by 6000BCE and cultivated in parts of southern Canada by 1000CE. Beans also originated in Central America and the Southwest. Maize, beans, and squash became such important staples that they were christened the "Three Sisters," and where they grew in abundance, populations thrived.

**LEFT** This Hopi wall-painting incorporates a variety of elements that represent agriculture, the elements, and crop fertility. There is colored corn and a large stalk, as well as the nurturing sun and rain-bringing clouds.

**Nez Percé women of the Plateau region played an important role in tribal life as gatherers of wild plants and small game. While they worked, they carried their babies on their backs in cradle boards similar to this one. The floral and plant motifs that decorate this board reveal the artist's reverence for nature. Cradle boards were usually made by women and presented as gifts to female relatives.**

In some tribes, the process of cultivating crops shifted economic and social control toward women, who were often responsible for planting and harvesting. The Iroquois believed that crops could not grow without female intervention, and this endowed their womenfolk with substantial power. Ceremonial life, which was centered on the agricultural cycle, was controlled by three societies: the Sisters of the Life Supporters performed planting ceremonies; the Sisters of the Three Life Sustainers enacted fertility ceremonies to promote plant growth; and members of the Women Planters Society conducted the Green Corn Ceremony at harvest time. Matriarchal lineages, called *ohwachira*, controlled property communally, including the longhouses in which the Iroquois lived, the fields, tools, and stored foods. Inheritance of everything, including seeds, went through the *ohwachira*.

As well as providing essential food, plants were widely used for healing (see page 116) and in ceremonies. In the deserts of the Southwest, the Maricopa and Tohono O'odham peoples gathered edible fruit from cacti such as the saguaro or nopal. The Tohono O'odham marked the start of the rainy season with a ceremonial drink made from this fruit. In many places, wild and cultivated tobaccos, considered to be soothing, were commonly used in rituals, usually by smoking it in pipes.

Plants also provided leaves and fiber to make netting and basketry. Yucca could be used as a soap, and strong fiber could stripped from its leaves. Cattail (*Typha*) leaves were transformed into exquisite baskets, woven sandals, and even duck decoys for use in hunting. In the Great Lakes, bark from birch and other trees was used to make beautiful baskets and canoe covers.

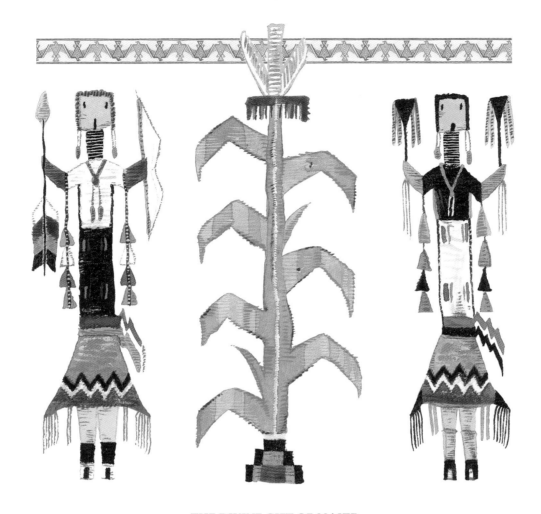

### THE DIVINE GIFT OF MAIZE

Across large regions of Native North America maize, or corn, is a staple crop that connects humankind and the gods—a divine link depicted in Southwestern arts in particular (above). Stories explain how the maize harvest was bestowed by Mother Earth figures—frequently called Corn Maiden or similar—to whom humankind repays its debt by conducting seasonal rituals to give thanks. This life-giving bounty has been developed into hundreds of colorful varieties (opposite), but even in the most conducive environments the fertility of the soil depends on favorable weather—and these conditions must be induced by prayers, which it is thought creatures such as butterflies (left and right) carry up to the gods.

# RITUAL AND SACRAMENT

Living in harmony with everything that Creator made requires constant observation. People who are properly respectful become connected to the sacred, thereby turning what they learn into "medicine" that has sacred power. This "medicine" may be as simple as a pebble found on a vision quest, which has become a personal talisman, or as complex as a knowledge of the stars learned over a lifetime, which reveals to a holy person the correct time to conduct the vital ceremonies that renew the world. Everyone should concern themselves with the way the world works so that they know when to perform the proper rituals and how to avoid giving offense. In this way, order is maintained in the world.

# THE WAY OF THE SACRED POWERS

People cannot know how sacred power, or "medicine," truly works, but almost every individual in traditional Native North American cultures knows something of its ways. Often seen as a force that is fluid, transmissible, and, importantly, malleable, sacred power can be manipulated by those who possess it—either for better or for worse. Anyone can have and use power to some degree: an ordinary individual may acquire it as part of a vision or dream; for example, he or she may find or be given an object that bestows medicine. Some Indians receive power at birth because of some physical characteristic—seen as a gift from the spirits—that makes them different from their peers.

Certain individuals, who are known as shamans or holy people, are seen as having especially strong links to the spirit world. Many complex rituals are designed to bestow sacred power on a person, to enable him or her to deploy it—or even to avoid being granted it, because not everyone welcomes the responsibility and danger that such power brings. Some seek power through fasting, self-torture, or through a vow made during a ritual. Solitude and suffering are thought to bring about more direct contact with power; thus, many holy people live apart from their community most of the time.

However they come by it, the chosen few need to learn how to use and control sacred power, often under the guidance of an elder holy person who may provide detailed training in the form of an apprenticeship or whose greater experience can be of help in interpreting spiritual messages. Holy people generally use their abilities to assist their people—for example, as healers (see page 116). Some use it to locate game, call animals, or deliver weather that promotes

LEFT This wooden figure with an opening in the chest was used by a member of the Ojibwe's Midewiwin sacred society, Leech Lake, Minnesota. The chest cavities of such spirit-imbued dolls usually contained charms belonging to a shaman.

ABOVE **Sunset Crater in Arizona, an extinct volcano sacred to the Hopi people. The Hopi believe that the wind god Yaponcha lives near the base of the cone. In March, when the wind is strong, Hopi chiefs and holy men make prayer offerings to Yaponcha.**

crop growth. However, shamans may occasionally choose to harm enemy individuals or groups by invoking disease or weather conditions that will harm crops.

In order to wield their power, holy people first have to connect with the spirit world. Some achieve this through chanting, dancing, or bodily deprivation. Others, such as a Yaqui holy man, might take datura or another hallucinogenic substance, and change into an animal spirit. Many rituals that involve the use of sacred power resemble a theatrical performance—one that is laden with symbolism. After receiving power, a Washo holy person needs to go to a recognized practitioner to learn ventriloquism, sleight of hand, and other skills needed for the "performance" part of the rituals he will be called upon to carry out for his people.

# HEALING WAYS

The most important task performed by Indian holy people is curing ill health. Almost all groups distinguish between everyday ailments, such as headaches or sore throats, and major illnesses, which are usually thought to be caused by the violation of important taboos or by more sinister forces, such as witches. Diagnoses and cures for serious woes almost always involve specialists who understand that wellness derives from balance in all aspects of one's life and that both the causes and cures of illness derive from the realm of the sacred.

Whenever a person becomes sick, a healer seeks the cause and tries to cure it, either by means of a solitary act or a community ritual. There are many forms of healing, from divination to herbalism. Divination ceremonies, during which a healer asks the spirits to reveal the cause of a problem, are often just a first step in the medicinal process, with other intermediaries involved in actually curing the illness. Some holy people are skilled at reversing spells cast by witches or driving out spirits in possession of a patient's body or soul. Such healers are often gifted psychologists, and many are also adept in sleight-of-hand and other important "people skills" that Western healers would refer to as "bedside manner."

Herbalism plays an important role in curing, and although many native people know plants that can be used to ease minor, day-to-day problems, learning which of the many available plants will remedy disease is a difficult task. Groups such as the Lenape seek specialists from among those people who feel an affinity for the plant kingdom. The Ojibwe find men and women who can communicate with plants, and these individuals become members of the Grand Medicine Society, or Midewiwin.

ABOVE  A Navajo *hatali*, or healer, beside a sand painting for one of the complex Chant Way healing ceremonies, which can last for up to nine days. The ceremony causes the spirits to make the painting their home and, if they are pleased, they will restore the patient to full fitness.

RIGHT  A Tlingit soul catcher made from a hollow tube of bone, decorated with figures of wild animals endowed with spirit power and inlaid with abalone shell. Soul catchers were among the most important objects used by a Northwest Coast curing shaman. Methods varied, but the tube might be placed on the affected body part to draw out an evil spirit, or used to blow away sickness.

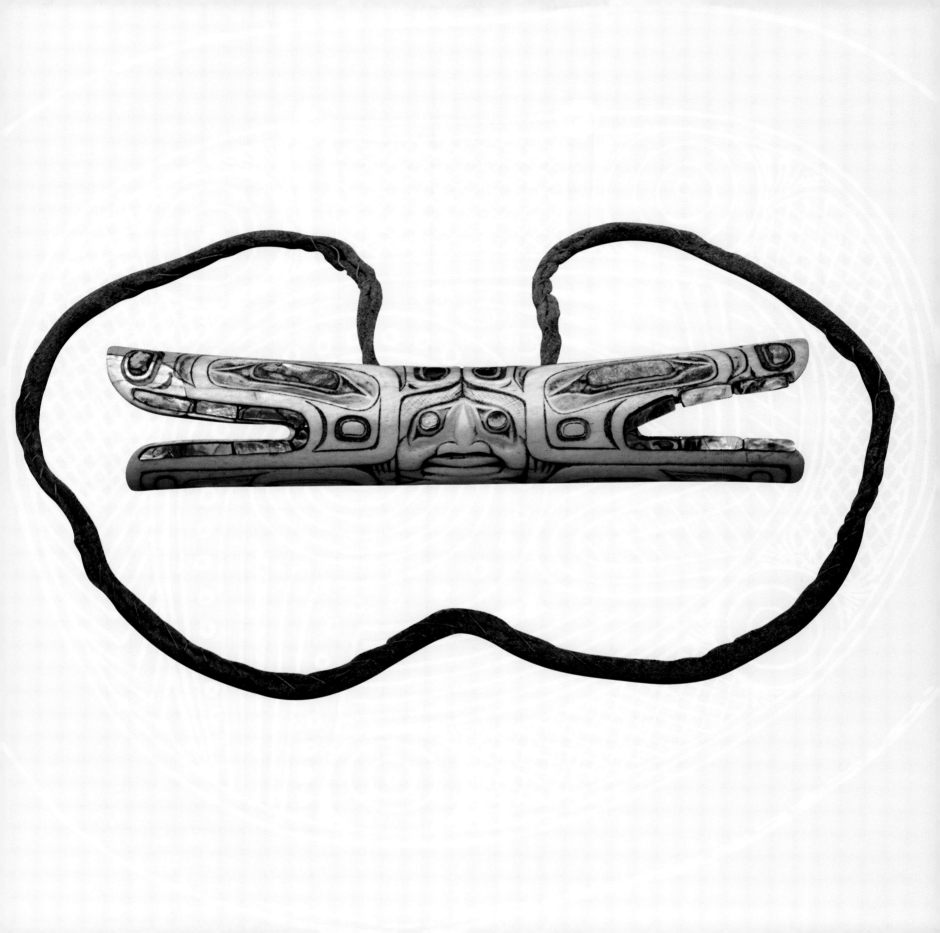

# SEEKING A VISION

Native people sometimes seek guidance from the spirits by way of visions, which usually occur during an altered state of consciousness. This condition can arise either as a consequence of illness, with a high fever and a loss of consciousness, or it can be induced. Visions may be brought on by depriving oneself of food, water, or sleep; by inflicting pain; by taking an hallucinogenic substance; or by dancing, chanting, drumming, or some other form of repetitive self-hypnosis.

The Pawnee word for vision means "to learn by being touched." An individual who experiences a vision while in a waking state or in a trance can usually see or talk to the powerful spirit, which may sometimes appear in concrete form, as an animal or ancestral being, but is more likely to be a nebulous "presence." Visions may reveal events of the past, present, and future, but usually they cannot be interpreted without help from a knowledgeable elder or holy person.

A vision is not always experienced as a blessing—some Indians try to deny or avoid visions because they often demand a response which the person is unwilling to give. However, vision quests remain a major part of religious practice for most Native North Americans, who draw on the power of the supernatural forces around them—at mountains and hilltops, at sources of water, in the depths of the forest, and even in areas where dangerous spirits dwell. An individual might embark on a number of vision quests during his or her lifetime. Commonly, the first vision quest is performed as a child nears puberty (although some cultures allow children as young as four to seek a vision), and the final quest might be undertaken in old age.

Vision quests require preparation, which usually means making oneself ritually and physically clean. This is accomplished by fasting and taking a purifying sweat bath—the intensity of each depending on the power of the vision being sought. For the Lakota, solitary vision quests are often conducted at the highest point in a

LEFT A Plains Indian Assiniboine hand drum painted with a spirit design that suggests a vision figure experienced during a hallucination, which may be induced by physical weakness and partial delirium as a consequence of fasting and thirsting.

locality. A small area of chosen ground might be marked out with stones and covered with sage or hide, accompanied by offerings such as strings of pouches of tobacco or strips of cloth representing sacred colors (see illustration page 26). Through good weather and bad, day or night, the individual fasts and prays until a vision comes or a spirit visits in the form of an animal. For many groups, vision quests are predominantly a male pursuit, but women can also "dream themselves power." In their visions women might acquire plants or charms to be used for healing or preparing food.

# CHANGE, RENEWAL, AND DANCE

Non-Indians often see the world of Native North Americans as timeless and unchanging, a view that could not be more mistaken. The Indian concept of time as cyclical rather than linear (see pages 92–93) means that both time and life are renewable, rather than being composed of a stream of events immediately exiled to the past. The key notions of change and regeneration are expressed in countless native rituals, from collective ceremonials of renewal to individual rites of passage.

In Native North American cultures, change is an element both of many ritual dances and of secular events such as powwows. For the Northwest Coast Kwakiutl, change was even built into the masks worn by some of the dancers (see pages 64–65). On the outside, transformation masks would be carved and painted with a clan totem or a key figure in a story reenacted as part of the dance. As the dance progressed, the dancer could pull strings, opening the mask to reveal another figure inside, thus literally transforming himself as a trickster or hero might do (see page 76). In some powwow dances, traditional dancers seem like men as they dance, then become prairie chickens or other animals. A hoop dancer might become an eagle, or the fringe on the grass dancer would turn him into the very grass on which he danced.

Nowhere is change more obvious than in the human life cycle, as naming practices demonstrate. Among the Cheyenne, a trusted elder, holy person, or grandparent carefully selects a name for an infant, often from a memorable experience or a dream. Childhood brings with it many changes in physical appearance, character, and deeds, and therefore a child may be given a new name as he or she grows up. Although in most tribes females kept their names for life, Cheyenne and Blackfoot males might have several through their teenage years, finally settling on a fixed name only in adulthood. For example, a young warrior who shot an enemy

RIGHT A Choctaw man dancing at a powwow in Phoenix, Arizona. His dance regalia contains a mixture of both Plains and Eastern Woodlands elements. Such regional combinations are now common sights and are indicative of the cultural changes that were wrought in the past as a result of forced relocation, and, more recently, due to intertribal powwows, which are part of a pan-Indian cultural renaissance today.

behind the ear might be renamed Behind the Ear. One who had spoken with the sun god in a dream might become Brings Down the Sun.

Earth-renewal rituals celebrate the completion of a cycle and are usually based upon the seasons, but can sometimes relate to longer natural patterns. These rituals often incorporate potent symbols of fertility and fortune for the group. For Plains tribes, the summer solstice is the major time of renewal and versions of the Sun Dance tend to play a key role in these celebrations. For other groups, first-food ceremonies are profoundly important because they celebrate fertility and mark the renewal of a subsistence cycle. For example, the Tsimshian people used to perform an annual ceremony to celebrate the appearance of the year's first salmon. The eldest holy people would go to the river to greet the fish. There, they would spread a cedar-bark mat on the ground, place some fresh salmon onto it, and carry it to the chief's house. A holy man dressed as a fisherman would lead the procession, waving an eagle feather in his right hand and a rattle in his left. Selected villagers attended the rest of the ceremony. A holy person would walk four times around the catch before preparing the fish for a ceremonial meal by cleaning each one with a mussel-shell knife (to use metal or stone would bring a violent storm). The fish were treated with such great honor because the respect shown would guarantee the salmon's return in the future.

Rites of passage mark important stages in the life cycle or changes in social status, such as when a person joins a sacred society. These are times of physical transition, and thus of great spiritual danger. Rites of passage usually include several segments: separation from those in a similar stage; liminality, when the person is between stages; and incorporation, when he or she becomes part of a new group. Incorporation might involve a test of endurance.

Rites may be simple, as when the Cheyenne pierce a child's ears to indicate his or her capacity to listen and learn; or they may be more dramatic, such as the rites

**LEFT A colorfully attired Zuni dancer performing in Albuquerque, New Mexico. The Zuni have a rich ceremonial life, some of it conducted in public and the remainder in private.**

that usually accompany the individual's passage into puberty. Adolescent males might be separated from their peers and sent for a time into the forest to fend for themselves, either to prove their manhood or to seek a vision. Female rites include those held at the onset of menstruation, which are filled with celebration and laden with symbols of fertility. Many tribes, including the Navajo, Tohono O'odham, and Wintu, have elaborate female coming-of-age rituals; for the Apache sunrise ritual, training begins about six months before the actual ceremony (see pages 124–125).

The Pomo of northern California performed ceremonies that encompassed the celebration of the first fruits, the initiation of the young, death and rebirth, and world renewal. At the core of these celebrations—known as Kuksu after the spirit who was both a culture hero and the Pomo First Man—was the creation of sacred time within the present. The festivities were led by members of four secret societies—Ghost, Hesi, Aki, and Kuksu—who wore elaborate regalia that imitated spirits and sacred animals.

BELOW **Pomo ritual ear ornaments such as these were used during the initiation of boys into manhood, which was one of the functions of the Pomo Kuksu cult.**

## FROM MAIDEN TO CHANGING WOMAN

Communal and individual ceremonies to celebrate the important milestones of a person's life are to be found in most cultures. In the southwestern United States, the cultural life of the N'dee or Western Apache is enriched by a variety of sacred rituals, of which perhaps the best known is the female puberty rite called the Naihes, or Sunrise Dance.

It is an arduous four-day-long ritual in which the participants re-enact the Apache origin myth about Changing Woman—also known as White Painted Woman—who gave birth to the tribe's culture hero twins: Slayer of Monsters, fathered by the sun, and Born of Water Old-Man, fathered by Water Old-Man.

During this time, the initiant girl makes the costume that she will wear to transform herself into Changing Woman, the tribe's first woman, whose life cycle she is imitating. The girl builds a lodge and strengthens herself for the task ahead. Her family gathers food and gifts to give away to those who participate in the ceremony. During the ritual itself, the girl is guided by her sponsor and a *diiyin*, or holy man. She dances for hours, with the number increasing each day, and must run toward the four cardinal directions to mark the four stages of life. Her sponsor molds her into Changing Woman by massaging her body. She is painted with sacred cornmeal, which she wears throughout the whole ceremony and must not wash off. On the final day, she blesses her people with pollen and provides healing and individual blessings for those tribal members who wish it.

# STATUS OF THE WARRIORS

Native Americans are often stereotyped as warriors, which is not to say that many were not; the point is that despite there being numerous sources of conflict between groups, and many men having considerable skill as fighters, wars of conquest with high numbers of deaths were a rarity. Although territorial disputes could cause violence, and some tribes maintain age-old rivalries today, raiding was the most common form of aggression. Forays were sometimes carried out in order to capture another group's women, who would then be made members of the raiding tribe. Expeditions might be organized simply for the honor and glory of participating in such a venture, with its attendant opportunities for prestige. This could be acquired by "counting coups" on an enemy—an act of extreme bravery involving a warrior getting close enough to an enemy to touch him with a hand or short coup stick (see illustration, left) without harming him and getting away again unharmed. But the post-Contact conflicts with Euroamerican colonizers introduced a new kind of warfare in which conquest rather than honor was the primary goal; and as settlers pushed into native lands, tribes were forced out into their neighbors' territories and the levels of intertribal conflict and killing increased.

Horses, which were introduced during the course of the sixteenth century (see pages 68–69), became both a means of waging warfare and a cause of it. Because they became sources of wealth as well as practical assets, the practice of raiding to capture horses developed, which further increased intertribal conflict. Some Indian groups achieved

LEFT **An elaborately beaded coup-counting stick collected from the Blackfoot in the 19th century. Coup sticks were used to touch an opponent in battle and most were quite plain. By the 20th century, more elaborate sticks had become common as part of powwow regalia and today's versions are called dance sticks.**

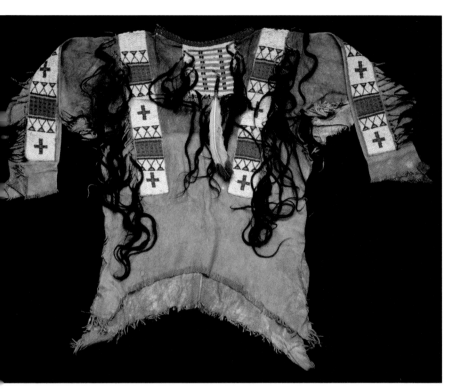

legendary status as horsemen. For example, by the late 1800s, the US Army considered the Cheyenne to be among the best light cavalry in the world.

In some native cultures, Indians achieved status as warriors as a result of having had many encounters with enemies in which they had acted heroically or used unusual and successful tactics; in other cultures men were born to the role of warrior. The Mohave had the *kwanami*s, or "brave men," a special class of fighters who received warrior powers from dreams that were said to begin in the womb. Such men were exempt from farming and domestic duties so that they were at liberty to wage war.

Warriors did not go into battle or on raids with their martial skills alone—they were also charged with spiritual power. For three days before a conflict, Chickasaw warriors would purify themselves by fasting until sunset, then drinking a purgative brew of snakeroot. Among many groups, the shaman conducted ceremonies and watched for bad omens to ascertain whether war plans had the blessing of the spirits. He sometimes went along on raids in order to use supernatural means to thwart the enemy, and might also treat wounds. Many communities held a war dance to boost the warriors' morale. Clothing and weapons might be decorated with a personal talisman for protection or to invoke success in battle (see pages 128–129). Afterwards, returning warriors might purge themselves by undergoing purification rituals.

LEFT A Plains Indian war shirt, intended to be worn during ceremonies rather than into battle. Shirts such as this one, with beaded or quillwork panels along the arms and shoulders, were associated with mature individuals who combined high warrior status with the role of diplomat— warriors known among the Lakota as "leaders of men."

## ADORNMENT OF THE BRAVE

Warfare in some Indian societies was as much a sacred undertaking as it was a pragmatic act of violence. Battle clothing was normally kept to a minimum so as not to impede movement: a breech cloth, a medicine bundle, and an eagle feather or two, as well as weaponry and a shield. However, the body itself would probably also be heavily adorned, perhaps with permanent geometric tattoos, or temporarily painted with colorful, highly personal designs on the face and torso that were believed to offer supernatural aid to the warrior. More elaborate garb for ceremonies might include a war shirt decorated with depictions of exploits in combat (above) or symbols of the attainment of supernatural force, such as bear power (left and right); or an eagle-feather warbonnet (opposite) to signify high status, perhaps earned by demonstrating bravery against the enemy.

## EXPLOITS IN BATTLE

Native North Americans have made pictographic records of events from their lives for thousands of years. The earliest tradition was what scholars call Ceremonial Art, attributed to those on vision quests or to shamans as part of ritual. Later, Biographic Art featured storylines of people's lives in action scenes, which included warfare and contact with Europeans and Americans. These forms of art made the transition from rock art to Winter Counts—hide paintings on which the key events of each tribe's year were documented. During the Reservation period, Indian agents and missionaries gave ledger-book paper and cloth to Indian warrior-artists so that they could document their own story or that of their tribe, and these individuals used the medium skillfully.

Recounting one's exploits in battle around a campfire was the prerogative of the great warrior, and such deeds were often recorded in the paintings. This work on muslin is by White Bird, a Northern Cheyenne and member of the Dog Soldier military society. It depicts a scene from Custer's last battle in 1876 at the Little Bighorn River, or Greasy Grass as it is known to the native tribes.

White Bird uses the imagery of horseshoes to show the battlefield movement of the combatants. Recent archaeological analysis of the site has revealed that Indian veterans of the fight essentially got it right in their first-hand accounts and drawings of the famous encounter. Custer's defeat was not a glorious last stand, but typical of battlefield disintegration when faced with overwhelming and terrifying odds.

# JOURNEY TO THE AFTERLIFE

Native North American beliefs about death and the customs and rituals surrounding bereavement varied from culture to culture. However, certain common themes do emerge—for example, most groups thought that the dead represented a danger to the living, and therefore the deceased were treated with considerable respect and caution. Although almost all native peoples believed in some plane of existence beyond the realm of the living, descriptions of the afterlife differed greatly, and the issue of what happens to the soul after death was a highly complex one for many Indian tribes.

When a person died, the greatest dangers were thought to be faced by the departed's close relatives. As a result, many cultures entrusted members of special societies or segments of the clan—composed of people considered to be the late person's more distant relatives—with responsibility for removing, cleaning, and disposing of the body, as well as getting rid of earthly goods, if that was required.

Many groups went to a great deal of trouble to avoid taking the body through the lodge's regular door in the belief that if the body exited by this route then those still living might soon follow in the deceased's footsteps. Sometimes the corpse was taken out through a window or the smokehole, or a new opening was created that would later be filled in again. Those involved in any way with the disposal of the body were careful not to offend the dead person and they ritually purified themselves after completing their duties.

It was widely believed that the dead were drawn back to where they had resided when alive. The Mohave and Yuma burned down the house of the deceased in order to prevent his or her ghost from trying to return there. The Navajo did not go to

LEFT **People of the Hopewell culture (ca.300BCE–500CE) placed lavish gifts in burial mounds. In addition to mica effigies such as this pendant in the shape of a hand, shell- and river-pearl ornaments and objects made of copper, stone, and bone were often interred with the dead.**

such lengths and simply abandoned the dwelling. In a similar vein, all the deceased's possessions might be given away to non-relatives, or even destroyed.

Some groups once believed that the body needed to be defleshed in order to be able to continue its journey, which created the specialist task of separating flesh from bones. More commonly this process was left to nature and bodies were placed on scaffolds or in trees and left to decompose. The resulting bones might be either left on the ground or gathered for burial, often in mounds (see pages 32–33).

Both scaffolds and burial mounds were sacred areas deemed by some to be spiritually dangerous. Among the Lakota *wanagi* ("things of the shadow") are spirits that guard graves and can harm anyone who disturbs the dead. However, other peoples do not see the remains of the dead in this way, but rather as objects to be cherished. According to these groups, for a set time after death the deceased continue to "live" near their relatives and need to be cared for. The Koyukon of Alaska maintain small houses where the body is placed and in which the late person's spirit resides for a period. After the winter has passed, the house is repaired or painted, and a favorite food of the deceased is burned in a fire so that the smoke can feed the dead.

Peoples who bury their loved ones often have special rituals. Such is the case with the Hopi who inter the

RIGHT **A Mimbres painted bowl from a grave in the Southwest. The hole has been punched through in order to permit the spirit to escape.**

dead in a sitting position facing west and surrounded by grave offerings. Some groups preferred cremation—the Luiseño of California used fire to release the soul into the sky, where it was thought it would become part of the Milky Way.

The rituals accompanying death may be as simple as taboos in which the name of the dead cannot be uttered or may involve public displays of grief. Among many Plains groups mourners cut their hair and wear it short for a year, slash their arms or chests, or wear mourning clothes. In some tribes, people make lengthy speeches to the spirit of the deceased and request that he or she stays away from the living.

Ideas about the afterlife differ widely, although none involves the "happy hunting ground" of the popular native stereotype. Much depends on beliefs about the human soul. The majority of tribes contend that each body has more than one soul, and assert that this is proved by dreams in which a person leaves his or her body and roams the world. At death, this soul might journey to the spirit world, while another might stay with the body until the mortal remains are burned or fully decomposed. Some Lenape believe in three souls: a blood soul that becomes a small ball and remains present in out-of-the-way places; a body soul that eventually joins the Creator to pass eternity in the afterlife after journeying through twelve cosmic layers; and a ghost that roams the Earth until the person it has once been passes out of the memory of the living. The Northwest Coast Quileute argue for five souls, with complex rules controlling their relationships in both life and death. Most native groups are agreed that the afterlife is out of the reach of the living.

One common vision of the afterlife sees it as a contrary realm where many things function in ways that are opposite to those with which the living are familiar. For example, rivers run backward, people dance with crossed feet, and seasons are mixed up. Among groups that believe in reincarnation, the afterlife is little more than a rest stop where the soul awaits its return to the world.

RIGHT **The gateway to the Nagmis (Nimpkish) First Nation Cemetery in Alert Bay on Cormorant Island, western Canada. Unusually, the remains of people from several different tribes are buried here. The graveyard is noted for its totem poles, many of which exhibit family crests and are memorial markers for deceased clan members.**

# SELECT LIST OF NATIVE PEOPLES AND REGIONS

Native North American tribal names can be confusing. Many names simply mean "the people," "the human beings," or "the real people"—an ethnocentric view of society that forged group cohesion. Names can reveal particular power relationships. A name that is in common use among Western historians and others may not have been used by the native people themselves. Some names were used by one tribe for another but were not complimentary. And a number of names were applied by Euro-American colonizers that were not necessarily approved of by "the people" themselves.

With hundreds of native nations and bands, it has been necessary to be selective by concentrating on those groups commonly written about. In the list, tribes appear by their pre-Contact culture area (see map, page 13). The first name cited (in **bold**) is the most common one, but it is sometimes followed by others. Where it is known or can be reasonably worked out, a transliterated version of the name used by the people themselves is given (indicated by the use of *italic* – or by ***bold italic*** if it is also the most common form in use). Where there is doubt over the derivation it is followed by a question mark (?).

## EASTERN WOODLANDS

**Abenaki:** Wabenaki, St Francis Indians
**Caddo:** *Kadohadacho*, Natchitoches (a confederacy), *Hasinai*, *Adai*, *Eyish*
**Cherokee:** *Ani-yun-wiya*, Tciloki
***Chickasaw***
***Chitimacha***
**Choctaw:** Chahta, *Pafallaya* (?)
**Cree:** *Ininiw*, *Nehiyawak*, *Atheneuwuck*, *Sackaweéthinyoowuk*
**Creek:** Muskogee (but comprised of many tribes)
***Seminole:*** *Miccosukee*,*Oconee*, *Yamasee* (several tribes)
**Deleware:** *Lenape*
**Fox:** *Meskwaki*, Mesquaki
**Huron:** *Wendat*, Wyandotte, Wyandot
**Iroquois:** *Kanonsionni*, *Haudensaunee* (a confederacy)
    ***Cayuga***
    **Mohawk:** *Kaniengehawa*
    ***Oneida***
    ***Onondaga***
    **Seneca:** *Onotowaka*
**Kickapoo:** *Kiwegapaw* (?)
**Menominee:** *Manomini*
**Micmac:** *Souriquois* (?)
**Ojibwe:** *Anishiabe*, Ojibwa, Ojibway, Chippewa, Mississauga, Slateaux
**Sauk:** Sac, *Oskaiwugi*
**Shawnee:** *Shawanwa*, Ouchaounanag, Chaouanons, Satanas, Shawano

*Wampanoag* (but also Pokanoket, Nauset, Sakonnet)
**Winnebago:** *Hochunga*, *Ho-Chunk*, Puants

## THE GREAT PLAINS

**Arapaho:** *Inuna-ina*
**Arikara:** Ree
**Assiniboine:** Stoney (in Canada), *U Sin*, *U Pwawa*
**Blackfoot:** *Pikuni* (Piegan), *Kainah* (Blood), *Siksika* (Blackfoot proper), *Sakoyitapix* or *Nitsitapix* (all)
**Cheyenne:** *Tse-tsehese-staeste*
**Comanche:** *Numinu*
**Crow:** *Absaroke*
**Hidatsa:** Gros Ventre, Minitari, Ree
**Kiowa:** *Ga-i-gwu*, *Ka-i-gwu*
**Omaha:** *Umon'hon*
**Osage:** *Ni-U-Kòn-Ska*
**Pawnee:** *Chahiksichahiks* (bands consist of *Panimaha* [Skidi], *Kitkehaki* [Republican], *Chaui* [Grand], *Pitahauerat* [Tappage])
**Sioux:** *Dakota*, *Lakota*, *Nakota* (signify three linguistic designations, but there are 13 subdivisions called *Oceti Sakowin* or Seven Council Fires)
**Wichita:** *Kitikitish*

## ARCTIC

**Alutiiq:** Aleut, *Sugpiaq*
***Inglulik***
***Inuit***
    **Baffinland Inuit:** *Nunatsiaqmiut*

**Caribou Inuit:** *Nunamiut*
**Copper Inuit:** Netsilik
**Labrador Inuit** or **Ungava:** *Inuit Kapaimuit*
**Inupiat**
*Unangan:* Aleut
*Yupik* or *Yup'ik*

**SUB-ARCTIC**
**Beaver:** *Deneza, Dunne-za*
**Carrier:** *Takulli*
**Chipewyan:** *Dene*
**Cree:** *Ininiw*, Muskegon, Woodland Cree
**Dogrib:** *Thlingchadinne*
**Hare:** *Kawchottine*
**Ingalik:** Deg *Hian*, Koyukon
**Kutchin** or **Gwich'in:** *Dindjie*
**Kaskapi / Montagnais:** *Nenenot, Innu*
**Slavey** or **Slave:** *Dinèè, Etchareottine*
**Tanaina** or **Dena'ina:** *Knaiakhotana*

**NORTHWEST COAST**
**Bella Coola:** *Nuxalkmx*
**Chinook**
*Haida*
*Kwakiutl:* *Kwakwaka'wakw, Kwakwala*
**Salish:** *Lummi* (Central Coast Salish), *Nisqually* (Southern Coast Salish), *Nooksak* (Central Coast Salish), *Puyallup* (Southern Coast Salish), *Quinault* (Southwestern Coast Salish), Comox or Catlo'ltx (Northern Coast Salish), *Suquamish* (Southern Coast Salish) and other bands
**Makah:** *Kwe-net-che-chat*
**Nootka:** Nootkans (?)

*Quileute*
*Tlingit*
*Tsimshian* (four main divisions: Coast, Southern, Nishga, Gitksan)

**PLATEAU**
**Coeur D'Alene:** *Skitswish*
**Flathead:** Salish, *Sèlic*
*Kalispel:* Pend d'Oreilles
**Klamath:** *Maklak*
**Kootenai:** *San`ka*
**Modoc:** *Maklak* (same as Klamath, who called them Moatokni)
**Nez Percé:** *Nimipu, Tsoop-Nit-Pa-Loo*
**Spokane, Spokan:** *Spoqèind*
*Umatilla*
**Yakama** or **Yakima:** *Waptailmim*

**GREAT BASIN**
**Shoshone** or **Shoshoni:** Wind River, Bannock (*Nomo*), Western (*Newe*), Gosiute
**Ute:** *Nunt'z*
**Paiute:** *Numa*
**Washo:** *Washiu*
**Yuma:** *Euqchan*, Quechan, Hokan

**SOUTHWEST**
**Apache** or **Chiricahua:** *Ndee, Dinèè* (includes Apache peoples or groups known as Cibecue, Lipan, Jicarilla, Mescalero, White Mountain, San Carlos, Mibreño, Northern Tonto, Southern Tonto)
**Colorado Indian Tribes**
**Havasupai:** *Pai*

**Hualapai:** *Pai, Walapai*
**Hopi:** *HopituhShi-nu-mu*
*Hopi-Tewa*
**Maricopa:** Pee-Posh, *Pipatsje*
**Mohave** or **Mojave:** *Tzi-na-ma, Aha-makave*
**Navajo:** *Dinèè, Dineh*
**Pima:** *Pi-nyi-match*, Akimel O'odham
**Pueblo:** Acoma, Cochití, Isleta, Jémez, Laguna, Nambe, Picurís, Pojoaque, San Felipe, San Ildefonso, San Juan, Sandia, Santa Ana, Santa Clara, Santo Domingo, Taos, Tesuque, and Zía
*Tohono O'Odham:* Papago
**Yaqui:** *Yoeme*
*Yavapai:* Enyaé Pai
**Zuni:** *Ashiwi*

**CALIFORNIA**
**Cahuilla:** *Iviatim*
**Chumash:** recent name, Santa Barbara Indians
**Hoopa** or **Hupa:** *Natinook-wa*
**Karok** or *Karuk*
*Maidu:* Konkow (Northwestern), Nisenan (Valley)
**Mission Indians:** (various groups, such as Luiseño)
*Miwok:* Tuolumne Me-Wuk
*Pomo*
*Shasta:* Konomihu, Okwanuchu, New River Shasta
*Yokut: Tachi Yokut, Choinumni, Chukchansi, Wukchumni*
**Yurok:** Olekwo'l
**Wintun:** Wintu (Northern), Nomlaki (Central), Patwin (Southern)

# FURTHER READING

Balikci, Asen. *The Netsilik Eskimo*. Waveland Press, Inc.: Prospect Heights, Illinois, 1989.

Basso, Keith H. *Wisdom Sits in Places*. University of New Mexico Press: Albuquerque, 1996.

Bierhorst, John. *The Mythology of North America*. William Morrow: New York, 1985.

Bruchac, Joseph. *Native American Stories*. Fulcrum Press: Golden, Colorado, 1991.

Chamberlain, Von Del. *When Stars Came Down to Earth: Cosmology of the Skidi Pawnee Indians*. Ballena Press: Los Altos, California, 1982.

Deloria, Vine, Jr. *God Is Red*. Dell Publishing Co., Inc: New York, 1973.

Downs, James F. *The Navajo*. Holt, Rinehart and Winston, Inc.: New York, 1972.

Dozier, Edward P. *The Pueblo Indians of North America*. Holt, Rinehart and Winston, Inc.: New York, 1970.

Echo-Hawk, Roger C. and Echo-Hawk, Walter R. *Battlefields and Burial Grounds: The Indian Struggle to Protect Ancestral Graves in the United States*. Lerner: Minneapolis, 1994.

Farrer, Clare R. *Thunder Rides a Black Horse: Mescalero Apaches and the Mythic Present*. Waveland Press, Inc.: Prospect Heights, Illinois, 1994.

Gill, Sam. *Mother Earth: An American Story*. University of Chicago Press: Chicago, 1987.

Hasselstrom, Linda. *Bison: Monarch of the Plains*. Graphic Arts Center Publishing Company: Portland, Oregon, 1998.

Keyser, James. *The Five Crows Ledger: Biographic Warrior Art of the Flathead Indians*. University of Utah Press: Salt Lake City, 2000.

Nelson, Richard K. *Make Prayers to the Raven: A Koyukon View of the Northern Forest*. University of Chicago Press: Chicago, 1983.

Pritzer, Barry. *Native Americans: An Encyclopedia of History, Culture, and Peoples*. ABC-CLIO: Santa Barbara, California, 1998.

Radin, Paul. *The Winnebago Tribe*. University of Nebraska Press: Lincoln, 1970.

Radin, Paul. *The Trickster: A Study in American Indian Mythology*. Schocken Books: New York, 1956.

Ridington, Robin, and Hastings, Dennis. *Blessing for a Long Time: The Sacred Pole of the Omaha Tribe*. University of Nebraska Press: Lincoln, 1997.

Sturtevant, William. (gen. ed.) *Handbook of North American Indians*. Smithsonian Institution: Washington, DC, 1981–2003.

Trigger, Bruce G. *The Huron*. Holt, Rinehart and Winston, Inc.: New York, 1969.

Versluis, Arthur. *Native American Traditions*. Element, Inc: Rockport, Massachusetts, 1994.

Woodhead, Henry. (series ed.) *The American Indians*. Time-Life Books: Richmond, Virginia, 1994.

Zimmerman, Larry J. and Molyneaux, Brian L. *Native North America*. Duncan Baird Publishers: London, 1996; and University of Oklahoma Press: Norman, 2000.

# INDEX

Page references to picture captions are in *italic* type.

## A

Abenaki people 76
Acoma people 41
Acumawi people 27
Adena Culture *33*
afterlife 132–134
agriculture 48, 53, 108–109
Aleut people *43*, 43
American Indian Movement 20
amulets 78–79
Anasazi people 10, *56*, 58, 92
    Chaco Anasazi people *97*
ancestors 63, 66–67
animals
    ancestral 66–67, 78
    in art 96, 97
    clan totems 18, 70
    in creation myths 42–43, 103
    masks *30*
    spirits 62
    *see also* individual species
Apache people 26, 47, 76, *113*, 123, 124
    creation stories of 90
Arapaho people 91
archaeology 12
architecture 8
    "big houses" 18
    cairns 55

circle motif 38, 93
cities 8, 14, 48–51
divination lodges 56–57
earth lodges 57, 93
*kivas* (chambers) 42, *56*, 57, 58
lodges *51*, 51–52, 93, 103
mounds 32–33
plank houses 52
spiritual concepts 103
*tipis* 38, 51–52, 93
Arctic region 15
Arikara people 51
art 16–18, *25*, 96–99
    Chilkat designs *70*
    records of events 130
    rock art 10, 94, 130
    sacred nature 96–97
    *see also* crafts
Assiniboine people *119*
astronomy 48–50, 92, 113; *see also* stars
Athapascan migration 47

## B

badgers 78
Badlands *41*, 103
basketry 16, *17*, *93*, 94, 109
beadwork 16, 96–97, *98*
beans 14, 48, 108
Bear Butte *26*, 27
bears 28–29, 66, 67
    Bear Dance *67*

clans 42–43, 70
    divine protection 78
    respect for 104
    warrior's bear power 128
beavers 91, 104
Beothuk people 8
Beringia land bridge 12, *15*, 41
Big Horn Medicine Wheel *48*
"big houses" 18
birds *see* under individual names
Black Hills 103
Black Wind (Apache creator god) 90
Blackfoot people 68, 93, 120, *126*
Blanco Peak 42
Blood Rock 27
body painting 128
Born of Water Old-Man 124
Bounding Bush ceremony 82
buffaloes 7, *25*, 30, 66, 104, 106
    link with the Lakota 75, *75*–76, 106
    skulls *51*, 52, 67
burial mounds 14, 32–33, 133
    restoration of grave goods 20

## C

Cahokia 48–51
Cahuilla people *93*
cairns 55
California region 15, 16
Canada 20, *22*
caribou 55

casinos 23
Catlin, George *46*, 67
ceremonies *see* rituals
Chaco Anasazi people *97*
Changing Woman 42, 124
    *see also* White Painted Woman
Chant Way healing ceremonies *116*
Chenoo monster 76–77
Cherokee people 37, 44, 70
    Booger Society 82
    White Peace Organization 82
Cheyenne people 47, 68, 75, 122
    as horsemen 127
    names 120
    sacred places *26*, 27, 29
Chickasaw people 127
Chilkat art *70*
Chippewa *see* Ojibwe
Chippewa-Cree Reservation 20
Choctaw people *46*, *120*
Christianity 8, 15, 57, 86
Chumash people 94
Cinder Cone *115*
circle motif 38, 92, 93, 94, *95*, 96
cities 8, 14
    Cahokia 48–51
clans
    origins 70
    totem animals 18, 70
Cliff Palace, Mesa Verde 58–59
clothing, for battle *127*, 128

Coast Mountain range 43
Coast Salish Indians *36*
Columbus, Christopher 15
Comanche people 68
Contact 17, 47, 126
Copper Inuit *see* Netsilik people
coups 126, *see also* warriors
corn *see* maize;
 *see also* Green Corn Ceremony
corn dance *53*
Corn Maidens 111
Corn Mothers 41
cosmogonies *35*, 35, 38, 51, 52
 *see also* astronomy; creation stories;
 stars
Coyote 62, 76, 90
cradle boards *109*
crafts *23*, 96–99
 basketry 16, *17*, *93*, 94, 96
 beadwork 16, 96–97, *98*
 *jewelry 96*
 pottery 16, 96–98
 quillwork 96–97, 99
 weaving *89*, 97, *99*, 99, 100
creation stories 40–43, 51, 90–91, 102
Cree people 30, 93, 104
cremation 134
crops 14, 48, 108–109
cross *see* motif
Crow people 67, 68, 70
crows 43
culture-area concept 15
culture heroes *see* heroes
Custer's Last Stand 130
cycles 92–93, 120–123

**D**
Dakota people *see* Sioux
dancing *8*, 16–17, *53*, 64, *87*, *113*
 Bear Dance 67
 corn dance *53*
 Eagle Dance 72
 in female puberty rite 124
 Ghost Dance 38, 86
 in hunting ritual 104
 "Matachines, Los" dance *87*
 in rituals of change and renewal
  120, *122*, 124
 Sun Dance *25*, 52, 86, 106, 122
 Sunrise Dance (Naihes) 124
 war dances 127
death 132–134
 *see also* afterlife; burial mounds;
  cremation
Devil's Tower (Mato Tipila) 28–29
Dineh people *see* Navajo
divination 116
 lodges 56–57
Dogrib people 27
dreams 80–81, 134
 dreamcatchers *81*
drums 38, 93, 118, *119*
ducks 43, 91

**E**
Eagle Dance 72
eagles 30, 43, 62, 67
 symbolism of 72–73, 128
Earth
 renewal rituals 122
 respect for 9, *30*, 61, *62*, 63, 113, 122

earthdivers 90–91
earth lodges 57, 93
Eastern Woodlands 15, 108
ecology 30, 104
 creation stories 40–43
 *see also* earth, respect for
education 23
effigy mounds 33
effigy pipes *32*, *62*
Elk Man 67
elk 67
*eloheh* (land) 44
emergence *see* origin stories
Europeans
 arrival in North America (Contact)
  *8*, 15, 30, 47
 missionary activity 15, 86
 wars with Native Americans 20,
  47, 130

**F**
False Face Society *82*, 82
Father Sky 9, 102–103
First Man and First Woman 42, 123
Flat Pipe 91
flood myth 43
Flute Ceremony 38
food *see* crops; *see also* individual plant
  names and animal species
Fox (Meskwaki) people 23, 47, 99
Fox 90
frogs *32*, 78

**G**
*ga'an* (mountain spirits) *113*

Galisteo Mountains *89*
gambling 23
geometric
 designs in craft 96–99
 mounds 33
Ghost Dance 38, 86
Gobernador Knob 42
gods, goddesses *see* individual names
Grand Medicine Society *see* Midewiwin
grave goods *132*
Great Basin region 15, 16
Great Lakes Indian Fish and Wildlife
  Commission 23
Great Plains region 15, 16, 51–52,
  106
Great Serpent Mound, Ohio *33*, 33
Green Corn Ceremony 109

**H**
Haida people 47, 52, 66, *116*
hallucinogens 86, 115, 118
Handsome Lake Movement 86
Harney Peak 36–37
healers and healing 82, 109, 114, 116
 *see also* individual societies
herbalism 116
heroes 74–76, 90, 124
Hesperus Peak 42
Hidatsa tribe 30, 93
Ho-Chunk people *see* Winnebago
holy men, holy persons *see* shamans
Hon'gashenu (Earth People) 35
Hopewell Culture *32*, *33*, *132*
Hopi people 38, 58, *61*, 92, *115*
 art *108*

burial rites 133–134

creation stories 41, 42

*kachinas* 57, *61*

*kivas* 56, 57

origins of clans 70

horses 61, 68, 126–127

horticulture 8, 14, 30, 108–109

housing *see* architecture

hunting 30, 81

buffalo 106

whales *63*

hunting/gathering 8, 14

Inuit 55

on horseback 68

rituals 93, *102*, 104, 106, 122

shamanic involvement 114

Hupa people 47

Huron people (Wendat) 42, 81, 99

**I**

Iktomi 27

Indian Gaming Regulatory Act (1978) 23

Indian Territory (Oklahoma) 44

*inipi* (purification ceremony) 56, 93

initiation ceremonies 82, 122–123, 124

Inshta-thuda (Sky People) 35

Inuit people 12, 34, 55, 62

animal spirits *62*

carving 99

dancing *113*

territory 20

totem animals 70

*inukshuks* (cairns) 55

Iroquois people *37*, 82, 86, 109

**J**

jewelry 96

**K**

*kachinas* (spirit beings) 57, *61*

Kiowa people *25*, *26*, 75

*kivas* (chambers) *42*, *56*, 57, 58

Kodiak Island 43

Koyukon people 34, 133

Kuksu cult *123*, 123

Kwakiutl people 64, 77, 82, 120

**L**

Lakota people 20, 51, 68, 86, 133

calendar 93

creation story 103

link with the buffalo *75*, 75–76, 106

primal power 62

reservation *22*

sacred places *26*, *27*, *41*, 118–119

sweat lodges 56, 93

thunder beings 36

landscape

culture-area concept 15

earth renewal rituals 122

relation to 7, 8–9, 44, 52, 89

sacred places 20, 23, *25*

wisdom places 26–29

*see also* individually named sites

languages 20, 23, 47

legislation 20, 23

Lenape people 116, 134

lodges *51*, 51–52, 103

divination lodges 56–57

earth lodges 57, 93

Lone Man 75

Luiseño people 134

**M**

maize 14, 48, 82, 108, 111

Mandan tribe 30, 75, 82, 104

*manitous* 62, 84

Maricopa people 109

masks *30*, 64, 82, 98, 120

Mato Tipila, Wyoming 28–29

Mattole people 47

medicine 113, 114–115

bags/bundles 35, 42, 63, 72, 128

people 63

wheels *48*, 51, 92

Mesa Verde National Park 58–59

Meskwaki people *see* Fox (people)

Micmac people 99

Midewiwin sacred society *114*, 116

migrations 46–47

Mimbres people 97, *133*

Mink (Trickster) 76

Mistassini Cree people *see* Cree

Mohave people 127, 132

monsters 76–77, 84, 103

*see also* individual names

Monument Valley *81*

moon 35, 38, 82

Mother Earth 9, 25, 61, 102–103, 108, 111

motifs,

circle 38, 92, 93, 94, *95*, 96

cross 51, 96

mounds 32–33, 48

Mount Shasta 27

Mount Taylor 42

mountains, sacred 41–42, 43

*see also* individual names, ranges

music 16, 17, *66*, 67

*see also* drums

muskrats 91

mythology *see* creation stories

**N**

Naihes *see* Sunrise Dance

Nakota people *see* Sioux

naming 120–122

Nanabush 76, 77

Narssuk 34

Native American Church 57, 86

Native American Graves Protection and Repatriation Act (1990) 20

Native North Americans

arrival in America 12–14, 46

displacement by Europeans 20, 44

diversity 8–9

ecological concerns 30, 104

economic hardships 22

languages 20, 23, 47

*see also* art; crafts

Navajo (Dine) people 10, *25*, 42, *61*, 132–133

coming-of-age rituals 123

healing *116*

origin story 47

Spider Woman *81*, *99*, 100

weaving *89*, *99*, 99

N'dee people 124

Netsilik people 34

Nez Percé people 90, *109*

Niagara Falls 36, *37*
nomadism 8, 48
Nootka people *63*
Northwest Coast region 15, 16, 18, 52
Nunavut 20

**O**
*ohwachira* (maternal lineages) 109
Ojibwe people 23, 25, 56–57, 76, 77
    bark lodges 103
        dreamcatchers *81*
        Midewiwin sacred society *114*,
        116
*okeepa* renewal ceremony 57
Old Man 68
Old Man Above 90
Omaha people 35
origin stories 27, 41–43, 47
    *see also* creation stories

**P**
Paha Sapa (Black Hills) 20, 36
painting, body *61*, 128
    tattooing 128
patterns *see* motifs
Pawnee people *51*, 51
performance arts 16–17
    *see also* dancing; music
petroglyphs 10, *61*, *89*
peyote 86
pictographs 10, 130
Pilot Mountain 37
plank houses 52
Plateau region 15
platform mounds 33, 48

Pleiades constellation 29, 35
pollution 30
Pomo people 108, 123
porcupine quills 16, 97
pottery 16, 96–98
powwows *8*, *20*, 93, *120*, 120
priests 50
protection *see* amulets
puberty rites 124
Pueblo Bonito *56*
Pueblo peoples 53, 57, 58, *86*, *87*, *97*,
    100, 104
puppets 82
purification
    ceremony (*inipi*) 56
    *see also* sweat baths, sweat lodges

**Q**
Qualla Indian Reservation 44
Quileute people 134
quillwork 96–97, 99

**R**
rabbits 67, 104
rattlesnakes *93*
ravens *43*, 43, 64, 76
Red Man 37
renewal ceremony (*okeepa*) 57
    *see also* dancing
reservations 22
rice 108
rites of passage 122–124
rituals 14, 33, 53, 63, 102
    agricultural 109
    Bounding Bush ceremony 82

burial 133–134
Chant Way healing ceremonies *116*
ceremonies of change and renewal
    57, 120–123
corn dance *53*
cycles 92–93
Flute Ceremony 38
Green Corn Ceremony 109
hunting 93, *102*, 104, 106
initiation ceremonies 82, 122–123,
    124
masks 64
New Moon ceremony 82
*okeepa* renewal ceremony 57
purification ceremony 56
Reconciliation Ceremony 82
role of sacred societies 82
shamanic 114
structures of 56–57
vision quests 118–119
warriors 127
    *see also* dance; music
rivers
    Colorado 42
    Little Bighorn 130
rock art 10, 94, 130

**S**
sacred places 20, 23, *25*
    mounds 32–33
    mountains 41–42
    wisdom places 26–29
sacred power 114–115, 118
sacred societies 82, 109, *114*, 116,
    122, 123

sacrifice *see* dance, rituals, visionary
    experiences
salmon 122
San Francisco Peaks 42
Saynday 75
Seneca people 86
shaking tents 56–57
Shalako Mana *57*
shamans 34, 52, 63, 67
    dolls, belonging to 102
    healers, in the role of *116*
    roles 102, 114–115, 127
    selection of 81
Shasta people 90
Shawangunk mountain range 84
shields 38, *39*, 79
Shiprock Peak *25*
Sierra Nevada mountain range 43
Sila 62
Sioux (Dakota, Lakota and Nakota
    peoples) 20; *see also* Lakota
*sipapu* (place of origin) 41, *56*
Sisters of the Life Supporters 109
Sisters of the Three Life Sustainers 109
Skidi Pawnee people *35*, 35, 102
sky 34–35
    spirits of *25*, 34, 35, 102
sky dogs (horses) 68
Slayer of Monsters 124
Smoky Mountain range 44
snakes 78, 93
social structures 8, 14, 48
    clans 18
    present-day trends 23
    sacred societies 82, 109

soul 134
soul catchers *116*
Southwest region 15, 16
squashes 14, 48, 108
Spider Rock 100
Spider Woman *81*, *99*, 100
spirit worlds 102–103
spirits
  earth spirits 35
  *ga'an* (mountain spirits) *113*
  grave guards (*wanagi*) 133
  *manitou*s 62, 84
  nature spirits 62–63
  sky spirits *25*, 34, 35, 102
  thunder beings *36*, 36–37
  *wegaleyo* 81
  *yei* spirits *89*
stars 34–35, 113
  Pleiades constellation 29, 35
  *see also* astronomy
story-telling 16
  *see also* creation stories; origin stories
Sub-Arctic region 15
sun 35, 38, 90
  dance, to honor the, *25*, 29, 52,
    86, 106, 122
  watchers, of the 92
Sunrise Dance (Naihes) 124
sweat baths 118
sweat lodges 26, 29, 56, 93
Sweet Medicine 27, 29, 75
syncretism 86

**T**
Talking God 100

Tanaina people *102*
*tatanka* (buffalo) 106
Tatqeq 34
Tecumseh, Chief 25
temples 33, 48
territories
  boundaries 33
  displacement by Europeans 20,
    44
  reservations 22
Tewa people 41
theatre 17
Three Sisters (crops) 14, 108
thunder beings 36–37
thunderbirds *36*, 62, 103
thunderstorms 34, 35
time and timelessness 52–53, 92–93,
  120
*tipi*s 38, 51–52, 93
Tirawahat *51*
Tlingit people *43*, 47, *70*, *116*
tobacco 109
Tohono O'odham people 109, 123
tools, stone 12, 16
totems 70
  animals 18–19
  art 16, 18–19
  poles 52, 98, *134*
trade 14, 99
Trail of Tears 44, *46*
transformative beings 66, 74
tricksters 62, 74–76, 90
Tse Bit'ai *see* Shiprock Peak
Tsimshian people *70*, 76, 122
turtles *91*, 91

**U**
Unkcheghila giants 103

**V**
visionary experiences *26*, 27, 29, 80,
  118–119

**W**
Wakan Tanka 62, 76
Wakinyan 36–37
*wanagi* (grave-guarding spirits) 133
war
  bonnets *128*
  dances 127
  practice of 126–131
  role of warriors in 126–128
  shirts *127*
Washo people 81, 115
weasels 67
weather 34, 114–115
  prediction 48–50
weaving *89*, 97, *99*, 99, 100
*wegaleyo* (spirit being) 81
Wendat people *see* Huron
whales 63
wheels, medicine *48*, 51, 92
White Bird 130
White Buffalo Calf woman *75*, 76, 106
White Painted Woman 124
White Peace Organization 82
Wichita people 93
Wind Cave, Black Hills 27
Windigo monster 76, 84
Winnebago (Ho-Chunk) people
  42–43, 70

Winter Counts 130
Wintu people 123
wisdom places 26–29
witches 116
women
  rites of passage 123, 124
  role of 97–98, 100, 109
  vision quests 119
Women Planters' Society 109
woodhenges 50–51
world view, Native American 8, 38,
  51

**Y**
Yagim monster 77
Yamosh 27
Yaponcha (wind god) *115*
Yaqui people 115
*yei* spirits *89*
Yellow Wind 90
Yokut people 43
Yuguk people *102*
Yuma people 132
Yupik people *30*

**Z**
Zuni people 53, 58, 78, 102

# PICTURE CREDITS

## PHOTOGRAPHIC CREDITS

The publisher would like to thank the following people, museums and photographic libraries for permission to reproduce their material. Every care has been taken to trace copyright holders; however, if we have omitted anyone we apologize and will, if informed, make corrections in any future edition.

Bridgeman Art Library, London/New York = BAL
Robert Harding Picture Library, London = RHPL
Werner Forman Archive, London = WFA

**Page 1** Corbis/Gerald French; **2** Corbis/Chris Lisle; **6** RHPL; **7** WFA/Glenbow Museum, Calgary, Canada; **9** Corbis/Kevin Fleming; **10** Indian Petroglyphs at Willow Springs, Tuba City, Arizona: Corbis/Tom Bean; **12** Corbis/Francis G. Meyer; **14** RHPL/Joe Cornish, Raleigh International; **15** RHPL/Walter Rawlings; **17** Corbis/Lindsay Hebberd; **18–19** Corbis/Gunter Marx; **21** John Running Photography, Arizona; **22** Corbis/Bob Rowan, Progessive Images; **23** Corbis/AINACO; **24** Corbis/CRD Photo; **25** Corbis/Stapleton Collection; **26** WFA; **28–29** RHPL/Dave Jacobs; **31** National Museum of the American Indian, New York City; **32** WFA/Ohio State Museum; **33** Corbis/Richard A. Cooke; **35** WFA/Field Museum of Natural History, Chicago; **36** WFA; **37** Corbis/Ron Watts; **38** *Tipi* under full moon in Colorado: Getty Images; **40** Corbis/Tom Bean; **43** Corbis/The Seattle Museum of Art, Washington; **44–45** Corbis/CRD Photo; **46** Art Archive/Chateau de Blerancourt/ Dagli Orti; **49** Courtney Milne, Arizona, USA; **50** Corbis/Tim Thompson; **53** Corbis/Richard A. Cooke; **54** Inuit cairn or Stacked Rocks, Baffin Island, Northwest Territories, Canada: Corbis/Galen Rowell; **56** Corbis/David Muench; **57** WFA/ Private Collection; **58–59** Getty Images; **60** Corbis/Catherine Karnow; **61** WFA/Robinson Museum, Pierre, South Dakota; **62** WFA/Alaska Gallery of Eskimo Art; **63** DBP Archive; **66** WFA/The Smithsonian Institution, Washington, DC; **67** Art Archive, London; **68–69** Corbis/Brian Vikander; **71** RHPL/Walter Rawlings; **73** Provincial Museum of Alberta, Edmonton, Canada (H65.84.1a-c, 2a); **74** Corbis/Jeff Vanuga; **77** McMichael Canadian Art Museum, Ontario; **80** Getty Images; **83** Corbis/Nathan Benn; **84–85** Getty Images; **86** Corbis/Craig Aurness; **87** Corbis/Danny Lehman; **88** Corbis/Arne Hodalic; **89** Corbis/ Christie's Images; **91** WFA/Field Museum of Natural History, Chicago; **92–93** RHPL/Walter Rawlings; **94** Chumash cave paintings, San Emigdiano Canyon, California: Corbis/David Muench; **97** Corbis/George H.H. Huey; **98** WFA/ Museum für Volkerkunde, Berlin; **99** Corbis/Christie's Images; **100–101** RHPL; **102** National Museum of the American Indian, New York City; **105** WFA/Plains Indians Museum, Buffalo Bill Historical Center, Cody, Wyoming; **106–107** Corbis/Layne Kennedy; **108** Corbis/Tom Bean; **109** RHPL/Walter Rawlings; **110** Indian Corn: Corbis/Steven Terrill; **112** Corbis/Kevin Fleming; **113** Corbis/ Arne Hodalic; **114** WFA/Private Collection; **115** Corbis/David Muench; **116** Corbis/ Arne Hodalic; **117** Corbis/Seattle Art Museum; **119** WFA; **121** Corbis/Buddy Mays; **122** Corbis/Danny Lehman; **123** WFA/Field Museum of Natural History, Chicago; **124–125** Steve Trimble Photography; **126** WFA/ British Museum; **127** Corbis/Christie's Images; **129** John Bigelow Taylor, New York City; **130–131** RHPL/Walter Rawlings; **132** Corbis/Richard A. Cooke; **133** WFA/Maxwell Museum of Anthropology, Alberqueque, New Mexico; **135** Corbis/George D. Lepp